Lisa Butterworth
& Amelia Wasiliev

Photography by Lisa Linder

28 Days Vegan

A complete guide
for beginners

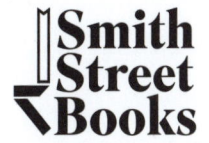

Smith Street Books

Smith Street Books

First published in French by Hachette Livre, Marabout division
58, rue Jean-Bleuzen, 92178 Vanves Cedex, France

This adapted edition for Five Below published in 2023 by Smith Street Books
Naarm (Melbourne) | Australia | smithstreetbooks.com
ISBN (Five Below Exclusive Edition): 978-1-92275-4-912

All rights reserved. No part of this book may be reproduced or transmitted by any person or entity, in any form or by any means, electronic or mechanical, including photocopying, recording, scanning or by any storage and retrieval system, without the prior written permission of the publishers and copyright holders.

Copyright © Hachette Livre, Marabout division, 2021

Editor: Ariana Klepac
Internal designer: Michelle Tilly
Cover designer: Murray Batten
Photographer: Lisa Linder
Stylist: Frankie Unsworth

Printed & bound in China by C&C Offset Printing Co., Ltd.

CONTENTS

INTRODUCTION — 04

BASICS, DRINKS & SNACKS — 06

28 DAYS OF MEALS — 54
  WEEK 1 — 56
  WEEK 2 — 72
  WEEK 3 — 88
  WEEK 4 — 104

RECIPE INDEX — 120

INTRODUCTION

In our modern society, humans have become hugely disconnected from our food, which is one of the main reasons we eat the way we do (i.e. terribly, for the most part!). We don't know where our food comes from (hint: it is not the supermarket), we don't know how it was grown or harvested, and when it comes to eating meat and dairy, we barely recognize that they come from animals.

We indulge in the bad stuff and skimp on the good, trading vitamins and nutrients for convenience and instant gratification. Although we ostensibly understand that what we eat affects our health, we have somehow lost our ability to listen to our bodies, and nourish them accordingly for optimal energy, immunity, resilience and wellbeing.

Eating a whole foods vegan diet addresses all of these issues, and that's just the beginning. Because veganism is more than just a diet – it is an ideology. It is a way of looking at the world and its inhabitants with utter compassion and wholehearted commitment, of treading lightly on the planet and honoring the bounty it provides, of nourishing ourselves fully, but not at the expense of living beings or our environment. Eating a cruelty-free diet often gets a bad rap. But that's starting to change, as people realize how empowering it is, and how much empathy it creates. It is not an overstatement to say that veganism can change the world. Plus, giving up animal products doesn't mean you will be relegated to sad salads, bland dishes or that most common of pejoratives: 'rabbit food'. Moving to a wholly plant-based diet means utilizing all of the incredible produce the seasons have to offer; getting plant-based protein from ethical, cruelty-free sources; and reaping the nutrients of ancient and whole grains. It means returning to an ancestral way of eating, rekindling our relationship to the earth and its natural bounty, and increasing our environmental stewardship by being intentional about what we put on our plates and in our bodies.

But deciding to go vegan, and successfully implementing a healthy, tasty, entirely plant-based diet, are two different things, which is why anyone curious about cruelty-free eating will find this book so useful. This book will walk you through 28 days of eating cruelty free – including a breakfast, lunch and dinner for each day, as well as snacks, drinks and sweets – with helpful weekly shopping lists and prep tips, to make your transition to a healthy, ethical, eco-conscious and, most of all, delicious way of eating, easy and enticing.

REASONS FOR GOING VEGAN

Deciding to go vegan is a very personal choice and the reasons for doing so will be different for everyone. But there are a few undeniable, overarching benefits of eschewing animal products in favor of a wholly plant-based diet. You might be driven by one more than another, but the good news is, you will reap (and sow) the benefits of each, all of which we will cover in more depth.

Improved health: Eating a whole foods plant-based diet has a number of well-documented health benefits, from the short term (like weight loss and lowered blood pressure) to the long term (decreased risk of certain cancers and heart disease).

Environmental concerns: Going vegan is the most effective lifestyle change you can make to personally reduce your carbon footprint and fight climate change on an individual level. Yes, slashing waste, cutting back energy use and reducing reliance on fossil fuels are all extremely important elements in the movement to slow the crisis but animal agriculture is the single-most environmentally destructive industry. Actively removing your support of it can make an immediate impact.

Animal activism: Perhaps your main reason for going vegan is simply to honor your love of animals and, to be honest, this is reason enough. Eating a wholly plant-based diet means no animals are hurt or killed in order to put food on your plate – a truly cruelty-free way to eat that you can feel good about inside and out.

ALL OR NOTHING?

If you eat a mostly plant-based diet, but can't seem to give up putting cream in your coffee, or indulging in some deli meats every once in a while, you probably can't technically call yourself a vegan. But *some* change is better than none, and you shouldn't let an all-or-nothing mentality prevent you from shifting to a sustained version of a healthy (almost) vegan lifestyle. Allow yourself a little flexibility if that's what helps you make the greatest, most long-lasting changes.

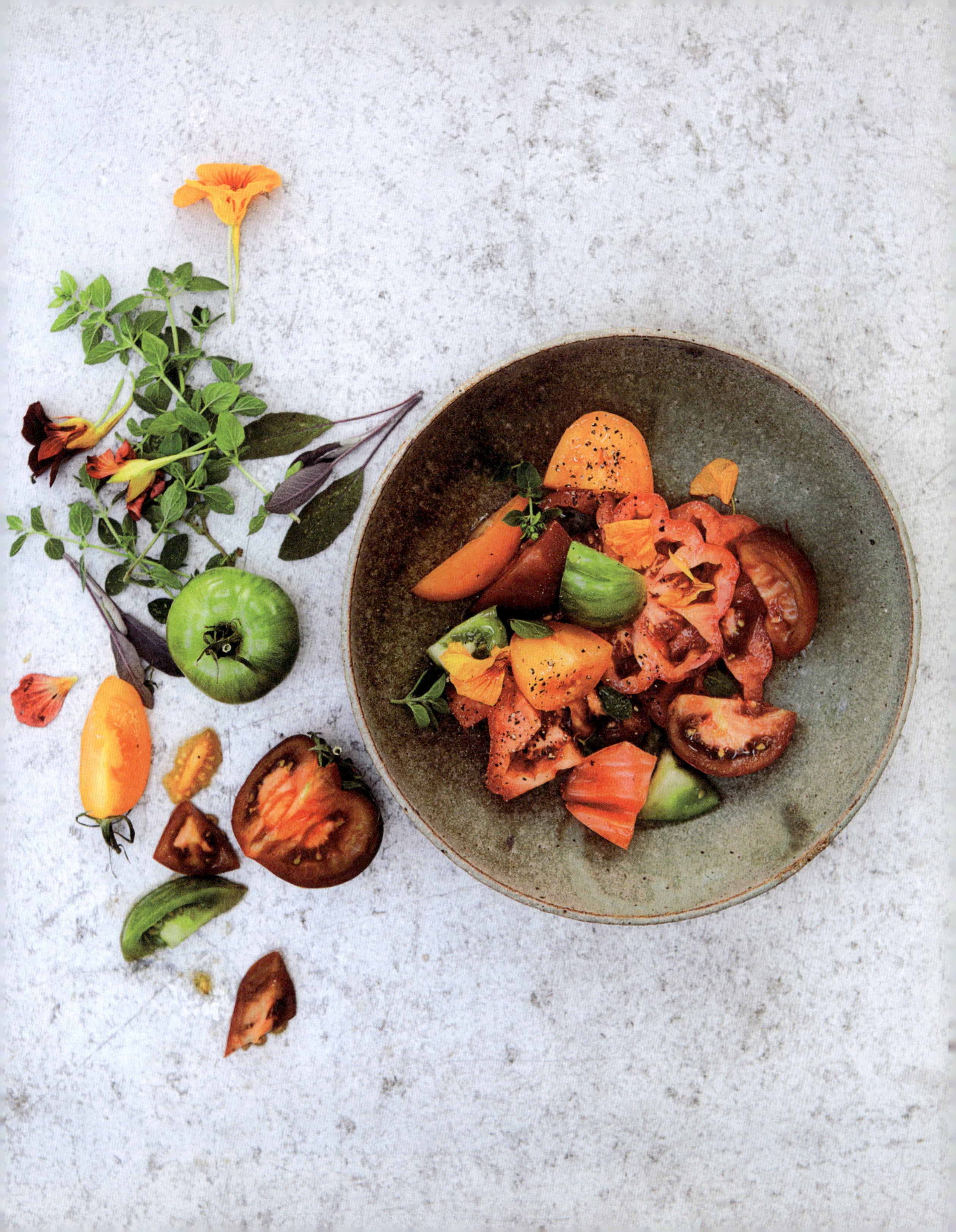

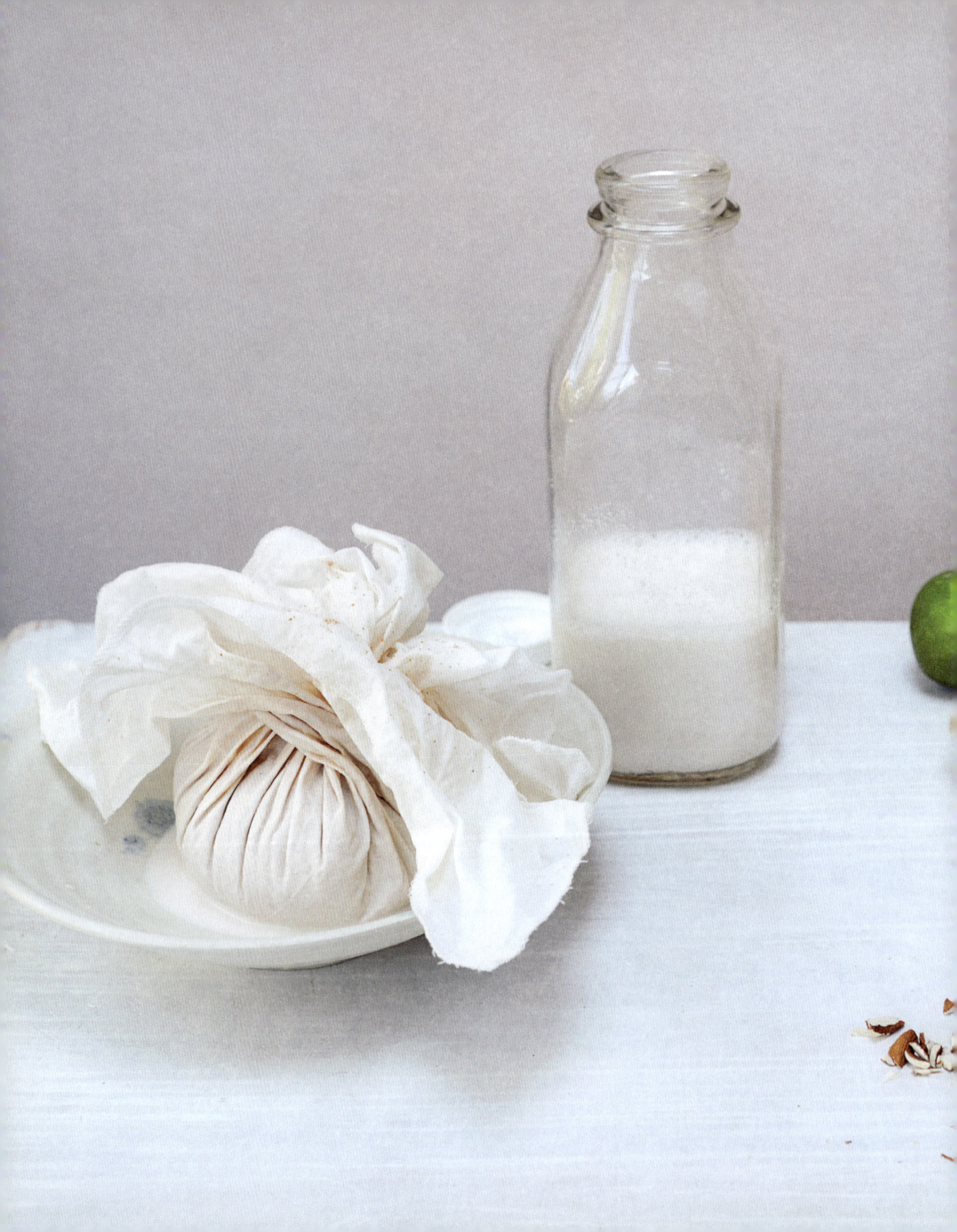

BASICS, DRINKS & SNACKS

If you are used to basing most of your meals on an animal protein, cooking vegan might feel like a challenge. This section will help make it easy. Recipes for foundational items such as grains, beans and stock, as well as flavorful dressings, spreads and vinaigrettes, will cover many of your major elements. The drinks and snacks recipes at the end of this section will help round out your culinary go-tos with a variety of small bites and beverages to satisfy every craving and make it easy to stick to your new way of eating. The recipes here are used throughout the 28 days of meals, and will certainly remain staples, whatever your ongoing diet entails.

NUT MILK & BUTTER BASICS

Nuts provide an excellent source of protein, healthy fats, fiber, vitamins and much more. They also boast a creamy quality. Nut milks and butters are very simple to make and can be used as a substitute for animal dairy products.

Almond milk

MAKES: 4 CUPS
PREP / SOAK TIME
10 minutes / 4–8 hours

5 oz raw almonds, preferably organic

Add extras for flavor too:
Maple syrup
Cinnamon
Dates
Unsweetened cocoa powder
Vanilla protein powder
Fresh berries

01 Place almonds in a small bowl and cover in water. Leave to soak for 4 hours, or overnight.

02 Drain almonds through a sieve, discarding soaking water, then rinse almonds and add to a blender with 4 cups water. Blend until smooth and creamy.

03 Line a fine-mesh sieve with muslin (cheesecloth), or use a nut milk bag, and place over a jug. Pour milk into sieve, then gather cloth around and twist to squeeze out all milk. Serve or pour into a bottle and chill in fridge for up to 4–5 days.

Nutrition per serve:
40 cals / 3g fat / 1g carbs / 2g protein

Oat & coconut milk
You can also use this same recipe to make oat milk using rolled (porridge) oats or coconut milk using coconut flakes. These won't need to be soaked though. You may need to adjust the fineness of your fabric so not as to let as much pulp through when straining and you may need to increase the amount of water.

Simple nut butter

MAKES: 1 CUP
PREP / COOK TIME
5 minutes / 10 minutes

10 oz almonds or use other nuts such as cashew nuts, macadamia nuts, hazelnuts and pecans (soaked/ sprouted have best benefits)

01 Preheat oven to 350°F. Spread nuts out on a baking tray and roast for 6–8 minutes until fragrant and golden brown. If roasting hazelnuts, rub in paper towel to remove skins before blending.

02 Add roasted nuts to a food processor and blend until smooth. Serve or store in fridge for up to 3 weeks.

Nutritional info is based on using almonds – per serving 1 tablespoon:
101 cals / 9g fat / 3.4g carbs / 2.4g protein

ALMOND MILK

SIMPLE NUT BUTTER

SPROUT BASICS

Sprouts are seeds that have begun to germinate. Sprouting increases the nutrient levels of the seeds and is helpful to our digestion. Sprouts tend to have higher protein levels so can be a great addition to a vegan diet. Many seeds can be sprouted and common sprouts that can be bought include mung beans, alfalfa, snow pea sprouts and bean sprouts... Here's how you can make your own at home.

HOW TO SPROUT:

01 Select a clean jar about 2-cup capacity. A wide top gives the seeds more space. Measure out the seeds or beans you wish to sprout, then rinse them under cold running water and drain.

- Smaller seeds (alfalfa, mustard, sesame etc.) – 3 tablespoons
- Larger beans (peas, mung beans, lentils) – 2¾ oz
- Larger chickpeas, almonds – 5½–7 oz per jar

02 Cover the seeds or beans with plenty of cold water and leave to soak for 4–8 hours.

03 Cover the top of the jar with muslin (cheesecloth) and secure with a rubber band. Make sure the fabric is open so air and liquid can pass through.

04 Invert the jar to drain the water out through the fabric. Leave the jar at a 45 degree angle with a tray or plate underneath it so that any extra water can easily run off.

05 Rinse the jar out with cold water twice a day. It is important to do this to stop slime and mold developing. Return the jar to its draining position in a cool place out of direct sunlight.

06 Continue step 5 for 3–7 days, depending on what you are sprouting. Judge when the sprouts are finished by the look and taste of them. Refrigerate and start eating them.

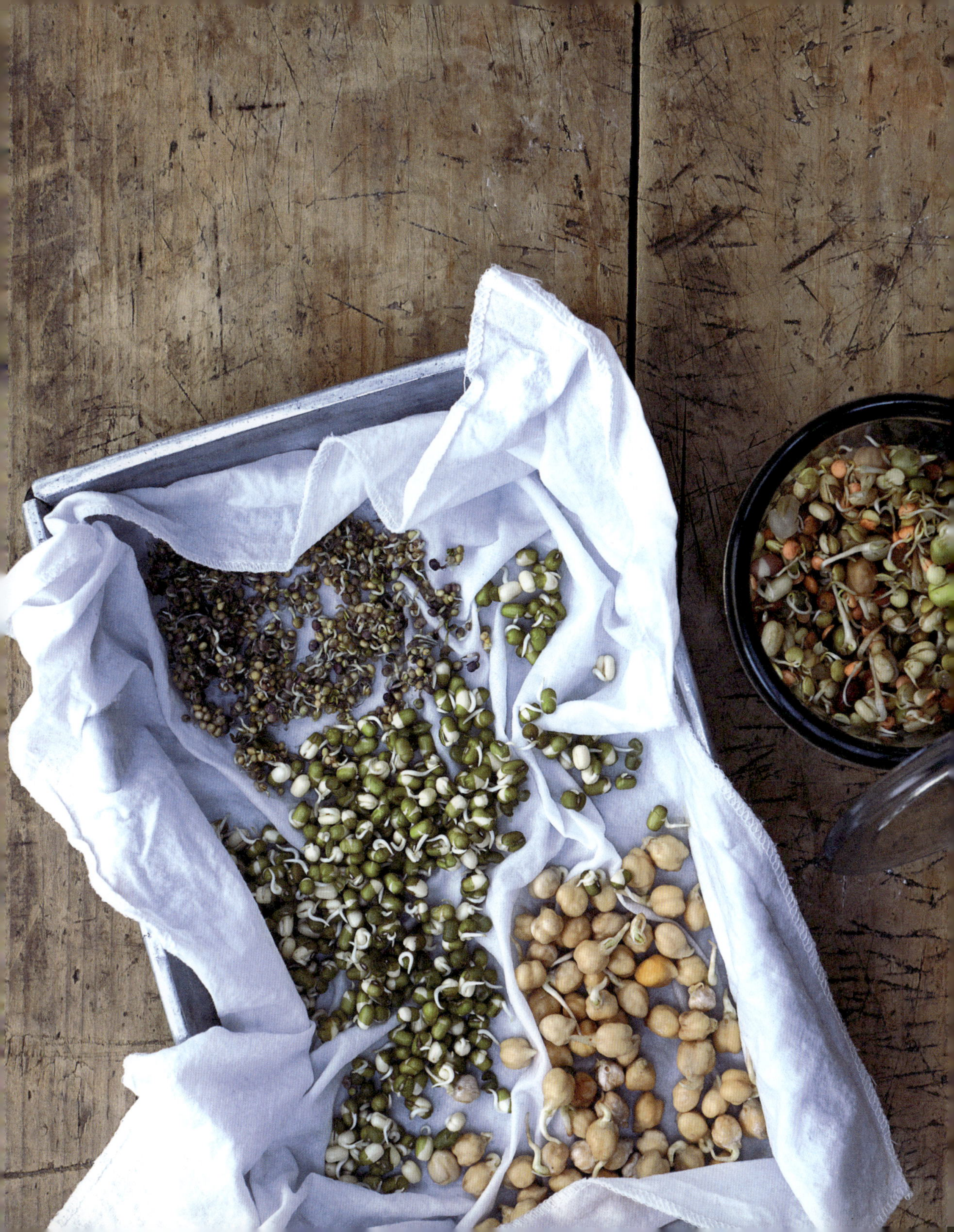

HOW TO COOK LEGUMES

While most legumes can be bought cooked and prepared in tins, there is a much larger variety available dried and it is really not difficult to prepare them. In fact, they can also be much more versatile.

A FEW BENEFITS OF USING DRIED BEANS/LEGUMES:
- Grind your own flours – use chickpeas, lentils, fava beans.
- Make sprouts.
- You can make sure they are soaked.
- The texture and flavor of the pulses and beans is much better.
- It is cheaper.

APART FROM LENTILS AND DRIED PEAS, ALL PULSES AND BEANS SHOULD BE SOAKED.

01 Select a clean jar about 2-cup capacity. A wide top helps the beans to have more space.

02 Cover the beans with 2–3 times their volume in cold water and leave to soak for 8–12 hours. (You can do a quick soak method by boiling the beans for 5 minutes, then leaving them in their boiling water for 2 hours.)

03 Rinse and drain the beans.

04 Place the soaked beans in a saucepan and cover with 2–3 times their volume of cold water. Add some flavoring if you like (garlic, onion, bay leaves, peppercorns). Bring to the boil and simmer for 1–1½ hours.

05 Use a slotted spoon to skim off any foam that forms while cooking. Drain when the beans are tender.

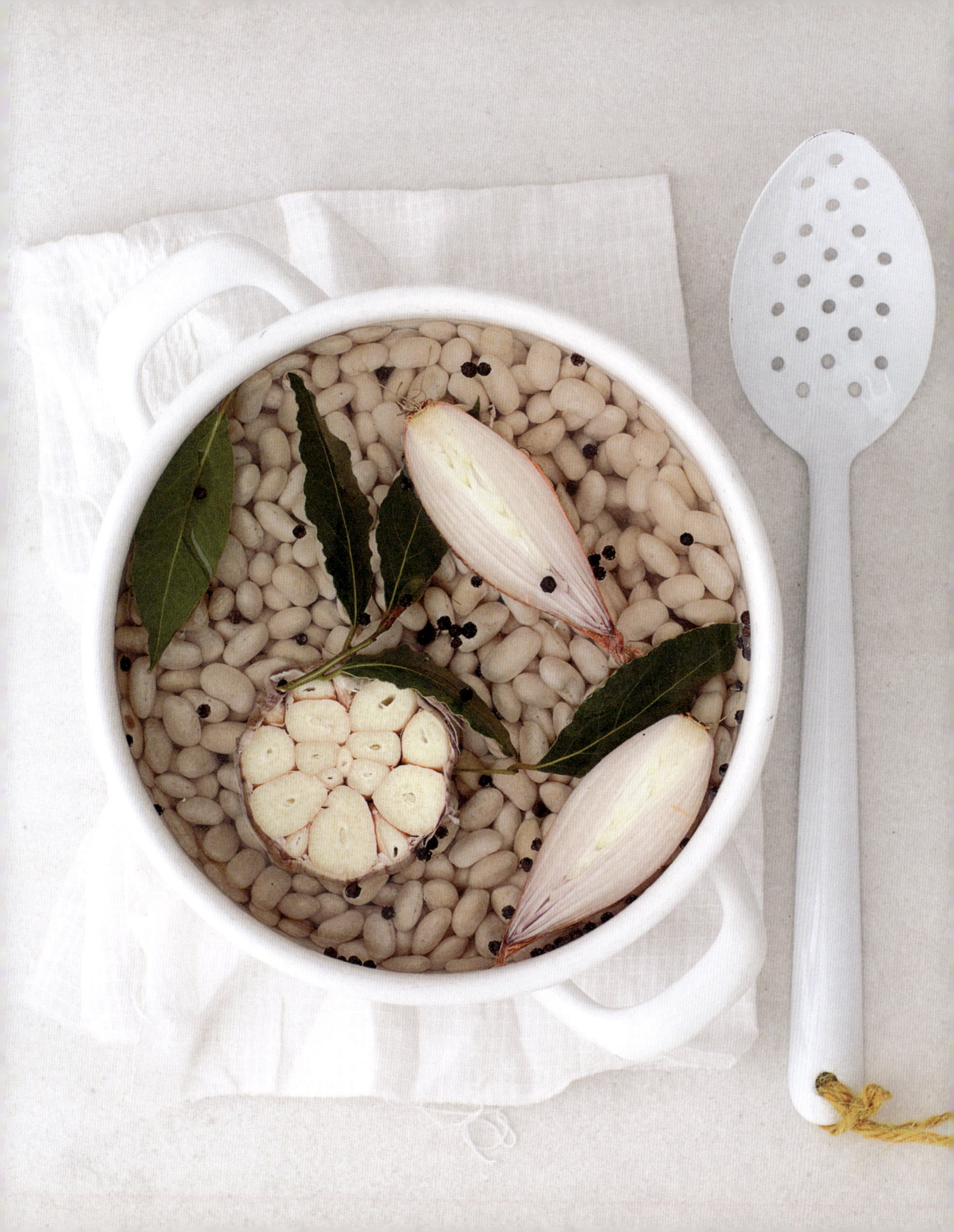

EGG ALTERNATIVES

Many standard recipes in baking and cooking call for eggs. Eggs are used in sauces and dips for creaminess, and in baking and desserts to bind and help lighten the mixture. There are a number of alternatives to eggs that can be used in many non-vegan recipes to create a similar outcome. Once you have tried a few you will realize that some alternatives are better than others for different recipes.

Chia seed egg

Great in baking and recipes where binding is necessary.

Substitute 1 egg for
   1 tablespoon chia seeds +
   3 tablespoons water

Mix chia seeds and water together in a small bowl. Leave to soak for 10 minutes before adding to your recipe as you would an egg.

Flaxseed egg

Substitute 1 egg for
   1 tablespoon ground
   flaxseeds + 3 tablespoons
   water

Whisk ground flaxseeds and water together in a bowl. Cover and chill in fridge for 15–30 minutes until it thickens. Use as you would to replace an egg in a recipe.

Aquafaba

Aquafaba is the cooking liquid from cooking legumes, most commonly chickpeas. It is best to start with using the liquid drained from a tin of chickpeas. Aquafaba whisks up very similarly to egg white so can be used in baking to aerate a mixture, or in desserts such as meringues. It is also used in cocktails to make a creamy foam or to make vegan mayonnaise and aïolis.

Substitute 1 egg for
   3 tablespoons aquafaba

Place aquafaba in a stand mixer and beat constantly for up to 5 minutes until stiff peaks form. It can help to get a stiffer mixture to add ¼ teaspoon cream of tartar. Use like this to replace an egg in a recipe.

FLAXSEED EGG

AQUAFABA

CHIA SEED EGG

VINAIGRETTE DRESSINGS

These dressings will keep in the fridge for up to 2 weeks. They are great to have on hand and add a zing to your salads.

Lemon mustard vinaigrette

MAKES: ½ CUP
PREP / COOK TIME
5 minutes / 0 minutes

½ cup olive oil
juice of 1 lemon
1 tablespoon apple cider vinegar
1 tablespoon dijon mustard
1 tablespoon wholegrain mustard
½ tablespoon maple syrup
1 garlic clove, very finely chopped
½ teaspoon salt
pepper

01 Combine all ingredients in a jar or jug and shake or whisk to combine.

Nutrition per serve:
120 cals / 12.62g fat /
1.9g carbs / 0.28g protein

Sesame rice wine dressing

MAKES: ½ CUP
PREP / COOK TIME
5 minutes / 0 minutes

juice of 1 lemon
2 teaspoons toasted sesame oil
3 tablespoons mirin
3 tablespoons rice vinegar

01 Combine all ingredients in a jar or jug and shake or whisk to combine.

Nutrition per serve:
100 cals / 9.1g fat / 5.46g carbs /
0.34g protein

Red wine vinaigrette

MAKES: ½ CUP
PREP / COOK TIME
5 minutes / 0 minutes

½ cup olive oil
3 tablespoons red wine vinegar
1 French shallot, finely diced
1 tablespoon dijon mustard
½ tablespoon maple syrup
½ teaspoon salt
pepper

01 Combine all ingredients in a jar or jug and shake or whisk to combine.

Nutrition per serve:
140 cals / 12.66g fat /
1.8g carbs / 0.8g protein

LEMON MUSTARD VINAIGRETTE

SESAME RICE WINE DRESSING

RED WINE VINAIGRETTE

CREAMY DRESSINGS

Creamy dressings are not missed in this vegan plan. Have one or more of these dressings on hand to add to salads or sandwiches. One can never have too much sauce.

Tofu miso dressing

MAKES: ½ CUP
PREP / COOK TIME
5 minutes / 0 minutes

1½ oz silken tofu
1 tablespoon white miso paste
juice of ½ lemon
½ teaspoon toasted sesame oil
1 teaspoon mirin
1 tablespoon toasted sesame seeds

01 Combine all ingredients in a blender with 1½ tablespoons water and blend until smooth. Make sure there are no lumps. Store in an airtight container in fridge for up to 7 days.

Nutrition per serve:
113 cals / 0.66g fat /
6.48g carbs / 5.58g protein

Coconut yogurt lime chili dressing

MAKES: ½ CUP
PREP / COOK TIME
5 minutes / 0 minutes

4 tablespoons coconut yogurt
juice of 1 lime
1 small red chili, finely diced, or ½ teaspoon chili flakes
salt and pepper

01 Add all ingredients to a jar or a small bowl with 2 tablespoons water and shake or whisk together until smooth. Store in an airtight container in fridge for up to 7 days.

Nutrition per serve:
88 cals / 7.49g fat /
6.21g carbs / 1.14g protein

Vegan aïoli

MAKES: ABOUT 1½ CUPS
PREP / COOK TIME
5 minutes / 0 minutes

3½ fl oz soy milk or 3 tablespoons Aquafaba (p.14)
1 garlic clove, crushed
7 fl oz–1 cup grapeseed or other vegetable oil
1 tablespoon apple cider vinegar
1 tablespoon dijon mustard
½ teaspoon salt

01 Blend soy milk and garlic in a food processor to combine.

02 While machine is running, slowly start pouring in oil, 1 tablespoon at a time, so oil is blending as it is added. As you add oil, it will start to thicken. Stop when you get to desired consistency. Add vinegar, mustard and salt and stir through. Store in an airtight container in fridge for up to 14 days.

Nutrition per serve:
221 cals / 24.45g fat /
0.8g carbs / 0.39g protein

TOFU MISO DRESSING

COCONUT YOGURT LIME CHILI DRESSING

VEGAN AÏOLI

PICKLES

Whether a quick pickle or a slower lacto-ferment, these are a great addition to your meals. Store in a cool, dark place for up to 4 weeks. Once open, store in fridge for up to 3 weeks.

Sauerkraut

MAKES: ABOUT 2 CUPS
PREP / FERMENT TIME
15 minutes / 2 weeks

14 oz (about ½ small) white cabbage, finely shredded, outside leaves reserved
1 fennel bulb, finely shredded
¼ oz dill, finely chopped
3 teaspoons salt

01 Place cabbage and fennel in a large bowl together with dill and salt and massage together with your fingertips for about 3 minutes. You will notice mixture becoming quite wet, as salt draws moisture out of cabbage and fennel.

02 Transfer mixture to a sterilized 2-cup capacity jar, pressing down firmly as you go to fit it all in. Use reserved cabbage leaves to sit on top and press down, making sure liquid is covering mixture. Push down on top layer so liquid from mix covers top of vegetables. Seal and leave in a dark place for 2 weeks. Check jar every couple of days and open and close lid to release any trapped gases.

Nutrition per serve:
20 cals / 0.12g fat / 4.69g carbs / 0.88g protein

Sweet pickled celery & fennel

MAKES: ABOUT 2 CUPS
PREP / COOK TIME
45 minutes / 10 minutes

⅓ cup agave syrup
1 teaspoon black peppercorns
1 teaspoon mustard seeds
4 cloves
1 teaspoon salt
½ cup white wine vinegar
3–4 celery stalks
1 small fennel bulb

01 Bring 1⅓ cups water and agave to the boil in a small pan. Add spices, salt and vinegar and simmer for 10 minutes to infuse.

02 Cut celery and fennel into bite-sized chunks and place in sterilized 2-cup capacity jar. (Save any remaining for end.) Pour hot liquid over celery and fennel to fill jar. Top with any extra chopped vegetables and more water, if needed. Cool. Serve or use baking paper to hold vegetables under liquid, then seal and chill.

Nutrition per serve:
25 cals / 7.49g fat / 6.21g carbs / 1.14g protein

Piccalilli

MAKES: ABOUT 2 CUPS
PREP / COOK TIME
4 hours / 25 minutes

5½ oz cauliflower florets
1 zucchini, diced
2¾ oz green beans, cut into small pieces
8 French shallots, quartered
1 tablespoon capers
1 cup white wine vinegar
1 tablespoon mustard powder
2 tablespoons all-purpose flour
½ tablespoon ground turmeric
½ tablespoon ground cumin
1 garlic clove, crushed
1 green apple, grated
3 tablespoons organic sugar
1 tablespoon mustard seeds
fine sea salt

01 Cover vegetables and capers with water and 3 tablespoons salt. Leave for 2–4 hours. Mix 3½ fl oz vinegar with mustard powder, flour and spices. Add 1 tablespoon vinegar to a hot pan and fry garlic and apple. Add rest of vinegar, sugar, pinch of salt and mustard seeds and boil. Whisk in paste. Simmer until thick. Drain vegetables, add to pan and heat briefly. Pack into jar.

Nutrition per serve:
40 cals / 0.42g fat / 8g carbs / 0.98g protein

SWEET PICKLED CELERY & FENNEL

PICCALILLI

SAUERKRAUT

CHUTNEYS

These chutneys are tasty additions to many meals and last in the fridge for 1–2 weeks.

Tomato & chili relish

MAKES: ABOUT 1 CUP
PREP / COOK TIME
5 minutes / 45 minutes

2 tablespoons coconut oil
1 onion, finely diced
4 ripe roma (plum) tomatoes
1–2 fresh red chilies
2 teaspoons dijon mustard
¼ cup malt vinegar
1½ tablespoons coconut sugar
salt and pepper

01 Heat oil in a pan over medium heat. Fry onion for 4–5 minutes. Add tomatoes and chilies and stir-fry for a few more minutes. Add remaining ingredients and reduce heat. Slowly simmer, stirring occasionally until tomatoes have cooked down and texture of sauce has thickened and become jammy.

02 Remove pan from heat and spoon mixture into a sterilized jar. Cool before sealing. Store in fridge for up to 4 weeks.

Nutrition per serve:
14 cals / 0.66g fat /
2.05g carbs / 0.19g protein

Eggplant caponata

MAKES: ABOUT 2 CUPS
PREP / COOK TIME
10 minutes / 25 minutes

2 small–medium eggplants, cut into chunks
2 tablespoons olive oil
1 red onion, sliced
2 celery stalks, sliced
2 ripe tomatoes, diced
2¾ oz green or black olives, pitted and halved
2 tablespoons red wine vinegar
2 tablespoons superfine sugar
2 tablespoons pine nuts, toasted
sea salt

01 Preheat oven to 350°F. Lay eggplant on a baking tray and drizzle with half the oil. Season. Roast until golden.

02 Meanwhile, heat remaining oil in a pan. Fry onion for 3–4 minutes. Add celery and tomatoes and season well. Add remaining ingredients and simmer for 5 minutes. Add eggplant to pan and stir. Store in airtight container in fridge for up to 1 week.

Nutrition per serve:
49 cals / 2g fat / 6.13g carbs /
0.9g protein

TOMATO & CHILI RELISH

EGGPLANT CAPONATA

TOPPINGS

These are great snacks on their own, but can also add extra texture to many dishes. Add some crunch to salads, curries or even breakfasts.

Crunchy seed mix

MAKES: ABOUT 1 OZ
PREP / COOK TIME
5 minutes / 5 minutes

2¾ oz pepitas (pumpkin seeds)
4 tablespoons sunflower seeds
2 teaspoons sea salt flakes
1 teaspoon vegetable oil

01 Heat a frying pan over medium heat. Add half the pepitas and half the sunflower seeds and toast for 2 minutes before tossing to make sure both sides of seeds are heated. Seeds will begin to make a popping sound and will become golden brown when ready.

02 Sprinkle with half the salt and half the oil and toss to coat. Cool seeds in a bowl. Repeat with second half of the ingredients. Cool before serving or storing in an airtight container for up to 1 month.

Nutrition per serve:
57 cals / 5g fat / 1.83g carbs / 1.9g protein

Candied nuts

MAKES: 4½ OZ
PREP / COOK TIME
5 minutes / 15 minutes

2 oz pecan halves
2½ oz raw cashew nuts
2 tablespoons maple syrup
pinch of salt

01 Preheat oven to 350°F. Toss nuts and maple syrup together in a bowl until nuts are coated. Sprinkle with salt. Spread out on a lined baking tray and bake for 10–15 minutes, stirring halfway through until golden. Make sure they do not burn.

02 Cool before roughly chopping to serve or store in an airtight container for up to 1 month.

Nutrition per serve:
75 cals / 6.16g fat / 4.69g carbs / 1.52g protein

Roasted sumac chickpeas

MAKES: ABOUT 15½ OZ
PREP / COOK TIME
5 minutes / 45 minutes

15½ oz chickpeas (tinned or cooked), drained (save liquid for Aquafaba, p.14)
½ tablespoon olive oil
1 teaspoon sea salt flakes
1½ teaspoons sumac

01 Preheat oven to 350°F. Make sure chickpeas are thoroughly drained. Transfer to a bowl and toss with oil, salt and sumac.

02 Spread out chickpeas evenly on a lined baking tray and roast for 40–45 minutes, shaking tray occasionally, until crisp and golden. Serve or store in an airtight container for up to 1 month.

Nutrition per serve:
215 cals / 4.17g fat / 34.62g carbs / 11.26g protein

CRUNCHY SEED MIX

CANDIED NUTS

ROASTED SUMAC CHICKPEAS

SPREADS

These spreads are great to have on hand for adding flavor and texture.

Pesto

MAKES: ABOUT 1 CUP
PREP / COOK TIME
10 minutes / 0 minutes

1 bunch of basil
2 oz toasted cashew nuts
1 teaspoon salt
1 garlic clove, roasted
¼–⅓ cup olive oil

01 Blitz all ingredients, except oil, in a food processor to combine. Add oil slowly, pausing once to wipe down side of bowl, then continue adding oil to achieve desired consistency.

02 Transfer to an airtight container with remaining oil covering top and store in fridge for up to 2 weeks.

Nutrition per serve:
81 cals / 8.15g fat / 1.65g carbs / 0.99g protein

Garlic whip

MAKES: 2 CUPS
PREP / COOK TIME
10 minutes / 0 minutes

2½ oz garlic cloves
1 teaspoon sea salt flakes
2 tablespoons lemon juice
10 fl oz grapeseed oil
2 tablespoons iced water

01 Cut garlic cloves in half, peel and remove center germ inside (small green bulb of regrowth).

02 Blitz garlic and salt in a food processor until garlic is minced, stopping to scrape down side of bowl occasionally. Add ½ tablespoon lemon juice and blend until a paste begins to form. Add another ½ tablespoon lemon juice and blend until mixture becomes lighter and slightly fluffy. While motor is running, slowly drizzle ¼ cup oil in a thick stream. Add next ½ tablespoon lemon juice, followed by another ¼ cup oil, then remaining ½ tablespoon lemon juice. Continue with ½ tablespoon water and ¼ cup oil until all water and oil has been incorporated. Chill in fridge in an airtight container for up to 3 weeks.

Nutrition per serve:
102 cals / 10.92g fat / 1.26g carbs / 0.23g protein

Tofu cream cheese

MAKES: ABOUT 1 CUP
PREP / COOK TIME
5 minutes / 0 minutes

7 oz block of extra firm silken tofu, pressed to remove extra moisture
2 tablespoons coconut oil
1 teaspoon apple cider vinegar
juice of ½ lemon
sea salt to taste
1 tablespoon nutritional yeast flakes

01 Blend all ingredients in a food processor or blender for 2–3 minutes until smooth. Taste and add more salt or lemon juice as needed. Chill in fridge for up to 5 days.

Nutrition per serve:
114 cals / 9.77g fat / 2.34g carbs / 6.04g protein

GARLIC WHIP

PESTO

TOFU CREAM CHEESE

SALSAS

These salsas use so many fresh herbs and are packed full of flavor and nutrition.

Pico de gallo

MAKES: ABOUT 1 CUP
PREP / COOK TIME
15 minutes / 0 minutes

½ red onion, finely diced
4 roma (plum) tomatoes, finely diced
1 fresh jalapeño, finely diced
1 bunch of cilantro, finely chopped
juice of 1 lime
sea salt

01 Mix all finely diced and chopped ingredients together in a bowl. Top with salt and lime juice and stir well to coat. Let mixture stand for 5–10 minutes for flavors to incorporate.

Note: If tomatoes are too ripe, it is probably best to remove seeds. Otherwise, just add it all together for more flavor. Store in fridge for up to 5 days.

Nutrition per serve:
22 cals / 0.2g fat / 4.91g carbs / 0.93g protein

Chermoula

MAKES: ABOUT 1 CUP
PREP / COOK TIME
10 minutes / 0 minutes

1 bunch of flat-leaf parsley, leaves and tender stems (about 1½ oz)
1 bunch of cilantro, leaves and tender stems (1½ oz)
½ bunch of mint leaves (about ¾ oz)
1 scallion
3 garlic cloves, peeled
juice and grated zest of 1 lemon
1 tablespoon red wine vinegar
½ teaspoon ground cumin
½ teaspoon smoked paprika
½–¾ cup olive oil
sea salt flakes

01 Blitz all ingredients in a food processor with a sprinkle of sea salt until well combined. Add more oil if needed to achieve a saucy consistency. Transfer to a jar and chill in fridge for up to 2 weeks.

Nutrition per serve:
60 cals / 5.94g fat / 1.62g carbs / 0.49g protein

Olive tapenade

MAKES: ABOUT 1 CUP
PREP / COOK TIME
10 minutes / 0 minutes

7 oz mixed pitted olives (black, kalamata and green Sicilian)
2 tablespoons capers
¼ cup olive oil
2 tablespoons lemon juice
½ oz flat-leaf parsley leaves, roughly chopped
1 tablespoon oregano leaves
3 thyme sprigs, leaves removed
1 garlic clove, chopped
6 large basil leaves
salt and pepper

01 Blend all ingredients in a food processor until smooth. Taste and add seasoning to your liking. Store in fridge for up to 2 weeks.

Nutrition per serve:
68 cals / 6.89g fat / 1.89g carbs / 0.35g protein

CHERMOULA

PICO DE GALLO

OLIVE TAPENADE

VEGAN BROTH

There are a number of vegan products you can buy that can save you making this broth but in most cases, homemade is best. The flavor is better and the freshness provides you with more nutritional benefits. You can save vegetable scraps and use them to make a batch as well. Have a container in the fridge at all times, then you can use in recipes as you need it.

MAKES: 14 CUPS
PREP / COOK TIME
10 minutes / 4 hours

- 4 shiitake mushrooms (fresh or dried)
- 2 large flat portobello mushrooms
- 2 pieces of kombu (dried kelp)
- 2 onions
- 1 large carrot, halved
- 1 garlic bulb, sliced in half horizontally
- 2 tablespoons vegetable oil
- 2 tablespoons white miso paste
- 2 celery stalks, plus leaves
- 3 flat-leaf parsley stems
- 1 tablespoon black peppercorns
- corn husks from 2 corncobs

01 Preheat oven to 350°F.

02 Combine mushrooms, kombu, onions, carrot and garlic on a baking tray. Whisk oil and miso together in a small bowl to a smooth paste. Drizzle over vegetables and roast for 40–45 minutes, stirring halfway through cooking.

03 Remove vegetables from oven and transfer to a large pan. Add remaining ingredients and 14 cups cold water. Cover pan with lid and bring to the boil. Reduce heat and simmer for 2–3 hours.

04 Let broth cool, then strain through a sieve to remove solids. Broth can be frozen for up to 3 months or chilled for up to 4 days.

Nutrition per serve:
62 cals / 2.76g fat / 0.8g carbs / 1.8g protein

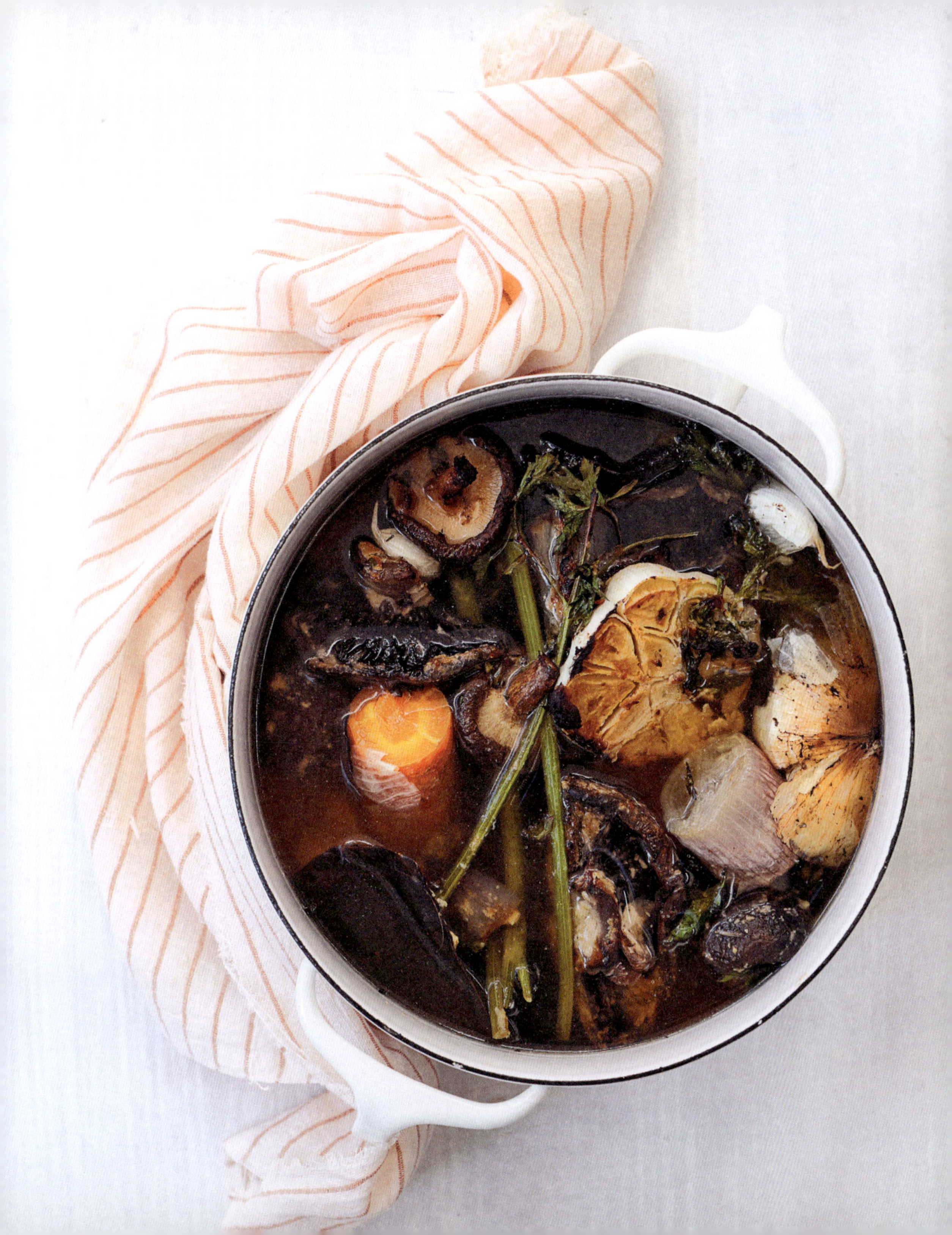

GRANOLA

Making a homemade granola is so easy. You can omit the sugar and add all your favorite ingredients. Add extras to the list below or swap out for something you prefer.

MAKES: ABOUT 12½ OZ
PREP / COOK TIME
10 minutes / 15 minutes

3½ oz rolled (porridge) oats
1½ oz coconut flakes
3 oz flaked almonds
1 oz dried cherries or cranberries
1 oz pecans, chopped
2 tablespoons sunflower seeds
2 tablespoons poppy seeds
2 tablespoons maple syrup
2 oz coconut oil

01 Preheat oven to 320°F.

02 Combine all ingredients in a large bowl and stir well to coat with maple syrup and oil.

03 Spread mixture out on a lined baking tray.

04 Bake for 15 minutes, stirring around halfway through cooking, until golden brown and toasted.

05 Leave to cool before storing in a jar or airtight container for up to 6 weeks.

Nutrition per serve:
121 cals / 6.91g fat / 16.8g carbs / 3.45g protein

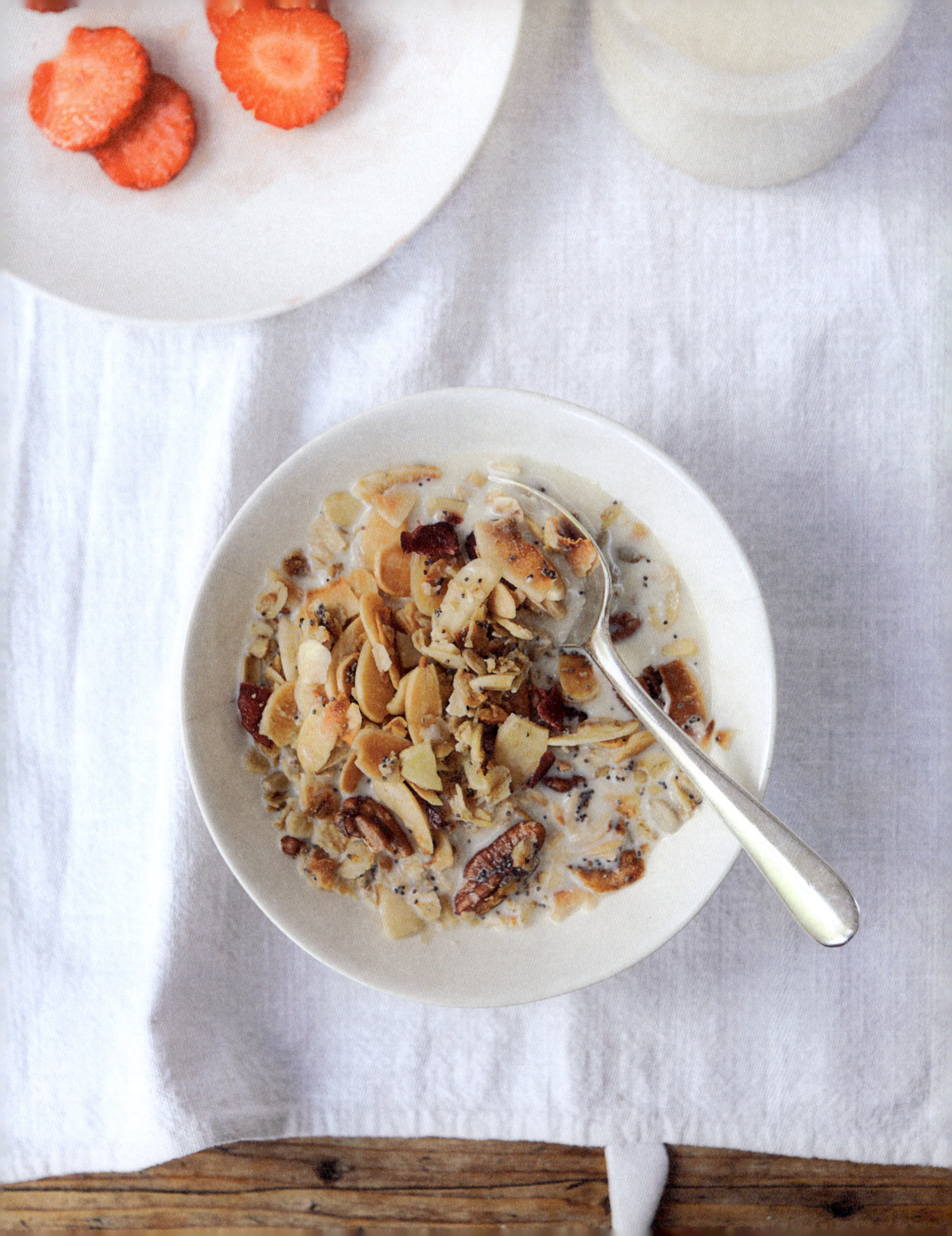

QUICK LOAVES

Store these loaves for up to 5 days or freeze individual slices, then toast them for a quick snack or a breakfast on the run.

Banana bread loaf

MAKES: 1 LOAF
PREP / COOK TIME
15 minutes / 50 minutes

2 Chia seed eggs (p.14)
6 oz self-rising flour
2 oz sesame flour
½ teaspoon baking soda
1 oz shredded coconut
2¾ oz raw (demerara) sugar
8 oz mashed banana
   (2–3 overripe bananas)
2¼ fl oz olive oil or coconut oil, plus extra for oiling
2 tablespoons maple syrup
1¾ oz coconut yogurt
2 teaspoons natural vanilla extract

01 Preheat oven to 320°F. Make chia eggs. Stir dry ingredients together. In another bowl, combine wet ingredients, then pour into dry ingredients and fold to combine. Pour into a lightly oiled 8-cup capacity loaf tin and bake for 40–50 minutes until a skewer comes out clean. Cool on a wire rack.

Nutrition per serve:
339 cals / 13.43g fat / 50.73g carbs / 7.22g protein

Carrot & parsnip loaf

MAKES: 1 LOAF
PREP / COOK TIME
15 minutes / 55 minutes

8 oz self-rising flour
½ teaspoon baking soda
2 carrots, grated (5½ oz)
1 large parsnip, grated
   (5½ oz)
5½ oz raw (demerara) sugar
¼ teaspoon ground cloves
¼ teaspoon ground nutmeg
1 teaspoon ground cinnamon
1 teaspoon natural vanilla extract
1¾ oz walnuts
5 fl oz nut or sunflower oil, plus extra for oiling
6 tablespoons Aquafaba (p.14)
¼ teaspoon cream of tartar

01 Preheat oven to 320°F. Blend all ingredients, except last two, in a food processor until smooth; place in a bowl. Beat aquafaba and cream of tartar to stiff peaks, then fold into mixture in the bowl. Pour into an oiled 8-cup capacity loaf tin and bake for 55 minutes until a skewer comes out clean. Leave for 10 minutes, then tip out onto a wire rack to cool.

Nutrition per serve:
418 cals / 13.43g fat / 48.67g carbs / 4.79g protein

CARROT & PARSNIP LOAF

BANANA BREAD LOAF

FLATBREADS

These are great simple recipes to have on hand. Use them to create a whole meal or as an accompaniment. You can experiment with both of these recipes, by adding different herbs and spices.

Chickpea flour crêpes

MAKES: 4
PREP / COOK TIME
5 minutes / 15 mins

3½ oz chickpea flour (besan)
1 teaspoon olive oil
salt and pepper
vegetable oil, for oiling

01 In a small bowl, whisk ingredients together with ½ cup water until smooth. The mixture should be quite watery, the consistency of normal crêpe recipe. Add a little more water if needed. Heat a nonstick frying pan over medium heat and coat the pan in oil. Pour a quarter of the mix in center of pan and lift and tilt pan so mixture spreads to cover base. Let crêpe cook for 2–3 minutes before flipping to cook other side. Remove from pan and repeat to make 3 more crêpes. Serve.

Nutrition per serve:
121 cals / 3.96g fat /
15.57g carbs / 5.77g protein

Quick flatbread

MAKES: 4
PREP / COOK TIME
10 minutes / 15 minutes

5½ oz all-purpose flour, plus extra for dusting
1½ oz chickpea flour (besan)
1 teaspoon fine sea salt
1 teaspoon baking powder
6½ oz soy or coconut yogurt
vegetable oil, for oiling

01 Mix ingredients together in a large bowl to form a dough. Use your hands to knead gently to form a soft ball. Dust a clean surface with extra flour and divide dough evenly into 4 balls. Knead each one slightly for a minute, then roll into a flat oval shape, about ½ inch thick.

02 Heat a griddle pan over high heat, brush with oil and cook flatbreads for a few minutes on each side, until dough puffs up and cooks. Serve at once.

Nutrition per serve:
203 cals / 1.7g fat /
38.45g carbs / 7.5g protein

CHICKPEA FLOUR CRÊPES

QUICK FLATBREAD

CRACKERS

These crackers are a great accompaniment to the dips (p.40), and make a simple snack on their own. Create more substantial lunches by adding some salad ingredients and avocado.

Chia seed crackers

MAKES: 20
PREP / COOK TIME
15 minutes / 45 minutes

mix of 1 oz flaxseeds and 1 oz hemp seeds
2¼ oz sesame seeds
2¼ oz chia seeds
2 oz pepitas (pumpkin seeds)
1 tablespoon nutritional yeast flakes
2 teaspoons tamari

01 Preheat oven to 300°F. Combine dry ingredients in a large bowl, stirring to mix evenly. Mix 7 fl oz water and tamari together, then pour into dry ingredients and mix well to combine. Let rest for 5–10 minutes. Mix again, then spread out over a lined baking tray. Smooth with back of a spoon, pressing down to ¼ inch thick.

02 Bake for 25 minutes. Remove from oven and cut into even cracker shapes. Turn crackers over and bake for 20 minutes, or until crisp. Store in an airtight container for 2 weeks.

Nutrition per serving:
1497 cals / 128.79g fat / 56.13g carbs / 57.07g protein

Rye snaps

MAKES: 20
PREP / COOK TIME
10 minutes / 20 minutes

2 teaspoons cumin seeds
1 teaspoon sea salt flakes
3 oz rye flour
3 oz all-purpose flour, plus extra for dusting
2 tablespoons toasted sesame seeds
3½ fl oz grapeseed oil

01 Preheat oven to 320°F. Grind cumin seeds and salt using a mortar and pestle. Combine with all other ingredients and 1 tablespoon water in a food processor and process until a dough is formed.

02 Knead on a floured surface for 3–4 minutes to form a smooth and not sticky texture. Divide and roll into a very thin sheet. Cut into your desired shape and carefully, using a butter knife, transfer to a baking tray. Bake for 20 minutes. Remove and let the snaps crisp further as they cool. Store in an airtight container for 2 weeks.

Nutrition per serving:
133.1 cals / 7.8g fat / 13.87g carbs / 2.20g protein

Olive oil crackers

MAKES: 8
PREP / COOK TIME
10 minutes / 8 minutes

4½ oz all-purpose flour, plus extra for dusting
1 oz semolina
¼ cup olive oil, plus extra for brushing
1 tablespoon sea salt flakes
1 tablespoon rosemary leaves, finely chopped

01 Preheat oven to 350°F. Combine all ingredients in a bowl with ⅓ cup warm water and stir to bring together. Knead dough on a floured surface for 6–8 minutes. Divide dough into 1 oz balls and use a rolling pin to roll out each ball into very thin tongue-shaped lengths. Lay 4 on a lined baking tray. Brush top of each cracker with olive oil and sprinkle with salt and rosemary. Bake for 8 minutes, or until golden brown. Repeat with remaining dough. Serve once cooled or store in an airtight container for 1–2 days.

Nutrition per serving:
113 cals / 5.26g fat / 14.22g carbs / 2.03g protein

OLIVE OIL CRACKERS

CHIA SEED CRACKERS

RYE SNAPS

DIPS

These dips make delicious snacks as well as great additions to meals. Eat the guacamole immediately, but the other dips can be stored in the fridge to add into dishes through the week.

Guacamole

SERVES: 4
PREP / COOK TIME
10 minutes / 0 minutes

2 ripe avocados
1 oz cilantro, finely chopped
2 French shallots, finely diced
2 red chilies, finely diced
juice of 1 ½ limes
salt

01 Mash avocados in a bowl, then add remaining ingredients and mix well to combine. Serve immediately.

Nutrition per serving:
177 cals / 14.88g fat /
12.59g carbs / 2.7g protein

Chargrilled eggplant & sumac dip

SERVES: 4
PREP / COOK TIME
10 minutes / 15 minutes

1 large eggplant
2 garlic cloves, finely diced
3 tablespoons tahini
juice of 1 lemon
2 teaspoons sumac
¼ oz flat-leaf parsley, finely chopped
1 tablespoon olive oil
salt

01 Turn flame of your barbecue or gas stove on and place eggplant directly over flame. Cook for a few minutes on each side until skin is blistered and eggplant is starting to soften. Place cooked eggplant in a bowl and cover. Cool slightly, then remove the skin. Combine eggplant flesh with remaining ingredients in a food processor. Season and process to your desired consistency. Serve or store in fridge for up to 1 week.

Nutrition per serving:
137 cals / 9.73g fat /
11.92g carbs / 3.47g protein

Beet hummus

SERVES: 4
PREP / COOK TIME
5 minutes / 0 minutes

14 oz tinned chickpeas, drained
1 small beet, roasted (see Warm beet & walnut salad, p.62)
1 garlic clove
2 tablespoons tahini
juice of ½ lemon
1 ¼ fl oz – ¼ cup olive oil
sea salt

01 Blitz all ingredients in a food processor. Add more lemon juice, salt and olive oil to taste and to achieve your desired consistency. Serve or store in fridge for up to 1 week.

Nutrition per serving:
255 cals / 21.09g fat /
13.55g carbs / 5.08g protein

BEET HUMMUS

CHARGRILLED EGGPLANT & SUMAC DIP

GUACAMOLE

SAVORY TASTY BITES

These tasty bites will help tide you over to your next meal and can each be kept close at hand so you can nibble when you need to. Store in airtight containers for 1 week.

Polenta fries

MAKES: 20
PREP / COOK TIME
4 hours 10 minutes / 15 minutes

2 cups Vegan broth (p.30)
5½ oz polenta
2 tablespoons nutritional yeast flakes
1 tablespoon finely chopped thyme and rosemary
sea salt flakes and pepper
vegetable oil, for frying

01 Bring broth to the boil in a pan. Use a whisk to stir broth as you gradually add polenta. Reduce heat and cook for 2 minutes. Stir with a wooden spoon as you see mixture thickening. Remove from heat and stir in yeast flakes and herbs. Season, then pour into a lined 8 inch square tin. Smooth and cover with baking paper. Chill for 4 hours or overnight until set.

02 Turn set polenta out and cut into ¾ inch fries. Heat enough oil for frying in a pan to 350°F. Deep-fry in batches for 5 minutes, or until golden brown. Drain and season.

Nutrition per serving:
102 cals / 6.98g fat /
9.2g carbs / 4.71g protein

Spiced roasted nuts

MAKES: 13½ OZ
PREP / COOK TIME
10 minutes / 45 minutes

2 teaspoons ground cumin
2 teaspoons smoked paprika
1½ tablespoons olive oil
2 teaspoons sea salt flakes
4½ oz macadamia nuts, roughly chopped
5 oz cashew nuts
5 oz almonds
1 oz pepitas (pumpkin seeds)

01 Preheat oven to 275°F. Mix spices, oil and salt together. In a large bowl, combine nuts and seeds. Add spice mix and stir until nuts are well coated. Pour mix into a lined baking dish, spreading it so the ingredients are evenly spaced and in a single layer. Roast for 30–40 minutes. Turn off oven but leave door closed and nuts in oven as it cools. This will help nuts to stay crisp as they cool. Once cool, transfer to an airtight container or serve.

Nutrition per serving:
282 cals / 27.27g fat /
7.71g carbs / 5.72g protein

Vegetable chips

SERVES: 4
PREP / COOK TIME
10 minutes / 20 minutes

2 curly kale stalks
7 oz sweet potato
3 tablespoons olive oil
sea salt and pepper

01 Preheat oven to 340°F. Remove stems of kale and cut leaves into large pieces. Use a vegetable peeler to peel thin strips off sweet potato. Rinse and dry kale leaves thoroughly. In a large bowl, pour oil over kale leaves and sweet potato strips. Massage oil into leaves and strips to cover well. Season and lay out on a lined baking tray, keeping vegetables separate.

02 Bake for 8–10 minutes until all leaves are crisp. Remove kale leaves and cook sweet potato for another 8–10 minutes until golden and crisp. Rest for 2 minutes before serving. Season more as desired. Best eaten fresh, but store leftovers in an airtight container.

Nutrition per serving:
265 cals / 20.38g fat /
19.6g carbs / 2.47g protein

SPICED ROASTED NUTS

VEGETABLE CHIPS

POLENTA FRIES

SWEET SNACKS

Even sweet treats can still be healthy if you choose good alternatives. These snacks are sugar free, but still have a high sugar content due to the dates and alternative sweeteners.

Salted caramel bliss balls

MAKES: 14
PREP / COOK TIME
15 minutes / 0 minutes

- 5½ oz finely shredded coconut
- 12 Medjool dates, pitted
- 1 tablespoon tahini
- 1 teaspoon natural vanilla extract
- 1 teaspoon sea salt flakes
- 2 tablespoons toasted sesame seeds or finely shredded coconut, for coating

01 Blitz coconut, dates, tahini, vanilla and salt in a food processor until chopped and well combined. Remove and roll into small balls, about 1 oz each. Coat in sesame seeds. Store in fridge for up to 2 weeks.

Nutrition per serving:
144 cals / 7.11g fat / 21.12g carbs / 1.52g protein

Granola bars

MAKES: 14
PREP / COOK TIME
10 minutes / 20 minutes

- 2¾ oz cashew nuts
- 1¾ oz almonds
- 4 oz macadamia nuts
- 1 oz goji berries
- 1½ oz chia seeds
- 1¾ oz sesame seeds
- ½ teaspoon sea salt
- 4 tablespoons coconut oil, melted
- 3 tablespoons maple syrup

01 Preheat oven to 350°F. Pulse all nuts and goji berries in a food processor until finely chopped. Tip into a bowl and add seeds, salt, oil and maple syrup. Pour into a lined 8 inch square baking tin and press down with back of a spoon. Bake for 20 minutes.

02 Cool for 30 minutes before removing from tin. Once cooled completely, cut into bars and serve or store in fridge for up to 2 weeks.

Nutrition per serving:
274 cals / 24.58g fat / 12.22g carbs / 5.08g protein

Chocolate peanut slice

MAKES: 16-20
PREP / CHILL TIME
20 minutes / 1½ hours

- 1¾ oz ground almonds
- 1 oz finely shredded coconut
- 2 oz unsweetened cocoa powder
- 6 Medjool dates, pitted
- pinch of salt
- 4 tablespoons melted coconut oil, plus 1½ tablespoons coconut oil (solid)
- 1 oz peanut butter
- 3 tablespoons maple syrup

01 Blitz ground almonds, coconut, half the cocoa, dates, salt and 1 tablespoon melted coconut oil in a food processor to form a dough. Press into base of lined 9 x 5 inch loaf tin. Freeze to set. Mix peanut butter, the solid coconut oil and 1 tablespoon warm water together until a pourable consistency. Pour on top of base and chill. Whisk remaining cocoa, maple syrup and remaining melted oil until smooth. Pour over filling and freeze for 1 hour. Cut into chunks. Store in fridge for up to 2 weeks.

Nutrition per serving:
255 cals / 16.54g fat / 25.15g carbs / 5.87g protein

SALTED CARAMEL BLISS BALLS

CHOCOLATE PEANUT SLICE

GRANOLA BARS

COLD DRINKS

It is nice to have a few options for an afternoon cool down. These drinks are refreshing and delicious. Black tea can be added to the ginger ice tea if you prefer a tea flavor.

Strawberry cordial

MAKES: 1 CUP
PREP / COOK TIME
5 minutes / 20 minutes

4½ oz strawberries, halved (tops included)
2¾ oz raw (demerara) sugar or an alternative
3 tablespoons lemon juice

01 Combine all ingredients in a small pan with 1 cup water and heat over low heat, stirring frequently until sugar is dissolved. Cover with a lid and simmer for about 20 minutes. Use back of a spoon to press strawberries to release their juices. Remove from heat, transfer strawberry liquid to a blender and blend.

02 Let liquid cool before storing in a jar or bottle in fridge. Use around ½ fl oz cordial to 10 fl oz sparkling or still water. Delicious with some ice, fresh lime and mint added too. Store in fridge for up to 1 month.

Nutrition per serving:
64 cals / 0.12g fat /
16.49g carbs / 0.22g protein

Ginger ice tea

MAKES: ABOUT 4 CUPS
PREP / COOK TIME
5 minutes / 10 minutes

2 lemongrass stalks, smashed
grated zest and juice of ½ lemon, plus slices to serve
1¾ oz piece of ginger, peeled and finely cut, a few slices reserved
1 tablespoon agave syrup

01 Combine all ingredients in a pan with 4 cups water. Cover and bring to the boil, stirring occasionally to mix. As soon as water has come to the boil, remove from heat and leave, covered, to steep for 5 minutes.

02 Strain and transfer into a bottle for storing. Place reserved ginger slices in bottle for extra flavor. Cool completely before serving over ice with a lemon slice. Store in fridge for up to 2 weeks.

Nutrition per serving:
122 cals / 0.58g fat /
31.52g carbs / 1.25g protein

Apple cider detox soda

SERVES: 1
PREP / COOK TIME
5 minutes / 0 minutes

juice of 1 orange
1 tablespoon apple cider vinegar
½ tablespoon agave syrup
1 cup sparkling water
lemon slice, to serve

01 Combine orange juice, vinegar and agave syrup in a glass. Stir well to mix thoroughly. Pour sparkling water into mix and serve with ice, if liked, and lemon slice.

Nutrition per serving:
55 cals / 0.12g fat /
13.42g carbs / 0.33g protein

Apple cider is known to offer various health benefits, including antimicrobial effects, aiding weight loss and lowering blood sugar levels. This drink is refreshing and packs a health punch at the same time.

STRAWBERRY CORDIAL

GINGER ICE TEA

APPLE CIDER DETOX SODA

HOT DRINKS

There's nothing better than a good cup of tea, morning, afternoon or evening. These hot drinks give you a daily boost with added health benefits.

Miso

SERVES: 1
PREP / COOK TIME
5 minutes / 5 minutes

10 fl oz Vegan broth (p.30) or water
1 tablespoon miso paste
1 teaspoon dried seaweed strips

01 Pour broth or water into a pan and bring to the boil. Remove a couple of spoonfuls of liquid and pour into a small jug with miso paste and whisk well until smooth. Pour back into pan and reduce heat to a simmer. Serve in a mug to sip with seaweed sprinkled on top.

Nutrition per serving:
35 cals / 1.03g fat /
4.66g carbs / 2.04g protein

Miso is a fermented food, so provides great soothing qualities for the gut and adds good bacteria. It is also full of essential minerals and vitamins.

Hot turmeric latte

SERVES: 1
PREP / COOK TIME
5 minutes / 5 minutes

10 fl oz almond milk (or any plant-based milk of your choice, p.8)
¼ teaspoon ground turmeric, or use ¼ oz turmeric root, sliced, if you have it
¼ teaspoon ground ginger
¼ teaspoon ground cinnamon, plus extra to serve
½ tablespoon maple syrup

01 Combine all ingredients in a small pan and heat over medium heat, stirring to thoroughly mix together. As the milk warms, whisk constantly to froth. Using a milk frother would be ideal if you have one. Once hot, pour into a large mug and sprinkle with extra cinnamon to serve.

Nutrition per serving:
30 cals / 0.05g fat /
7.83g carbs / 2.19g protein

Turmeric is a powerful anti-inflammatory and antioxidant. It is a soothing and calming addition to your day.

Fennel tea

SERVES: 1
PREP / COOK TIME
10 minutes / 0 minutes

½ tablespoon fennel seeds
1 tablespoon fennel fronds
10 fl oz boiling water

01 Crush seeds using a mortar and pestle. Place in a teapot along with fennel fronds, cover with boiling water and stir well. Leave to steep for 8–10 minutes. Strain into a teacup and drink.

Nutrition per serving:
30 cals / 1.29g fat /
4.55g carbs / 1.37g protein

This is a great tea for after meals, as it aids in healthy digestion and can be known to treat bloating and cramps.

FENNEL TEA

MISO

HOT TURMERIC LATTE

HOW TO: COOK BROWN RICE
(FOR RECIPE SEE DAY 1, P.58)

1. Measure and rinse rice of your choice. Generally 6½ oz of brown rice makes about 14 oz–1lb 5 oz of cooked rice, depending on variety.

2. Add rice to a pan with double the volume of water i.e., 6½ oz of brown rice to 2 cups of water.

3. Bring to the boil, reduce heat, cover and simmer for 35–40 minutes. Check water, there should only be a small amount.

4. Once rice is tender, take off heat, cover and steam for 10–15 minutes. Fluff rice with a fork before serving.

HOW TO: MAKE FLATBREADS
(FOR RECIPE SEE P.36)

1. Mix all ingredients in a large bowl and stir to combine.

2. Knead quickly to bring together to form a dough.

3. Roll dough out into 4 even oval shapes.

4. Cook on an oiled griddle pan for a few minutes each side.

HOW TO: MAKE ALMOND MILK
(FOR RECIPE SEE P.8)

1. Soak almonds in water overnight.

2. Drain and rinse almonds.

3. Combine with water in a blender and blend.

4. Strain through a nut milk bag and store milk in fridge for 4–5 days.

HOW TO: SOAK PRUNES
(FOR RECIPE DAY 25, SEE P.112)

1. Place dried prunes in a small heatproof bowl.

2. Boil water.

3. Pour boiling water over prunes to cover. Leave to stand as the water cools.

4. Cover and place in fridge. Store for up to 3 weeks in fridge.

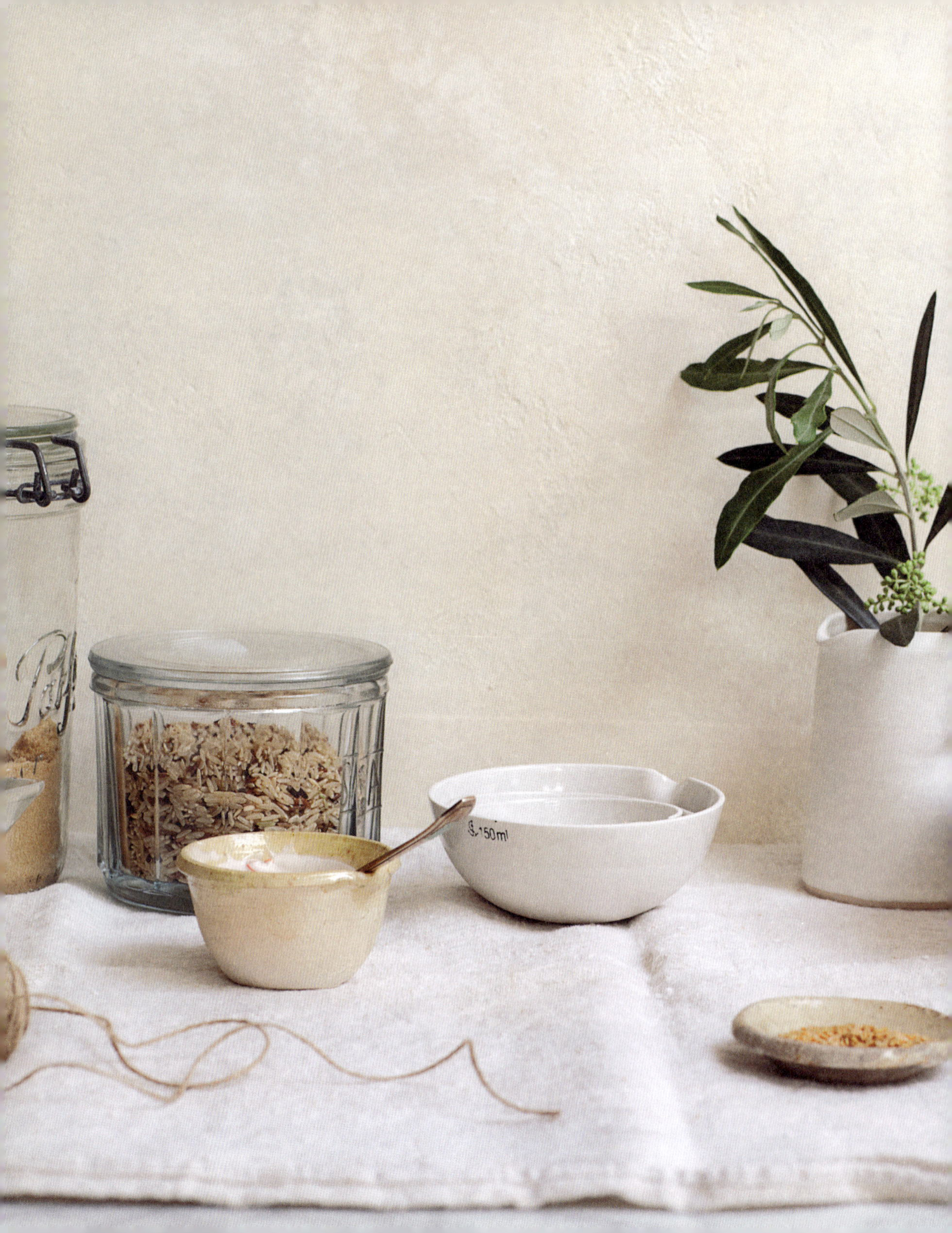
150 ml

28 DAYS OF MEALS

....

Whether going vegan is a gigantic shift for you, or simply a modest adjustment to your current mostly vegetarian way of eating, this section will ensure your success, at least for the next four weeks. These recipes are organized by day, with colorfully delicious meals including breakfast, lunch and dinner set for 28 days. Each week includes a shopping list as well as prep tips — many meal elements can be made ahead of time, so that you can spend more time enjoying your food than you do preparing it each day.

WEEK ONE
WEEKLY SHOPPING LIST

FRUIT & VEG
- [ ] basil – 2 bunches
- [ ] roma (plum) tomatoes – 3
- [ ] mixed heirloom tomatoes – 1 handful
- [ ] ruby red grapefruit – 1
- [ ] flat-leaf parsley – 2 bunches
- [ ] dill
- [ ] chives
- [ ] rosemary
- [ ] large portobello mushrooms – 2
- [ ] mint – 2 bunches
- [ ] cilantro – 2 bunches
- [ ] scallions – 4
- [ ] red onions – 2
- [ ] brown onion – 1
- [ ] lemongrass – 1 stalk
- [ ] red bell pepper – 1
- [ ] garlic – 2 bulbs + 7 cloves
- [ ] ginger – 2½ inch piece
- [ ] lemons – 4–5
- [ ] Persian cucumber – 1
- [ ] eggplant – 1
- [ ] baby spinach leaves – 8 oz
- [ ] arugula – ½ oz
- [ ] blueberries – ¼ oz
- [ ] beansprouts – 2½ oz
- [ ] red cabbage – 3½ oz
- [ ] butter lettuce
- [ ] French breakfast radishes – 2
- [ ] sweetcorn – 1 cob
- [ ] potatoes – 2
- [ ] carrots – 2
- [ ] parsnip – 1
- [ ] peach – 1
- [ ] avocados – 2
- [ ] sweet potato – 1
- [ ] bok choy – 1 head
- [ ] broccolini – 1 bunch
- [ ] banana – 1
- [ ] beets – 2

CHILLED/FROZEN
- [ ] nut milk – 7½ fl oz
- [ ] soy yogurt – 7 oz
- [ ] coconut milk – 1 cup (or nut milk)
- [ ] extra firm tofu – 1lb 1 oz
- [ ] coconut yogurt – 3½ oz
- [ ] frozen mango – 3½ oz

CHECK TO SEE IF IN PANTRY
- [ ] silken tofu – 1¾ oz
- [ ] rolled (porridge) oats – 1¾ oz
- [ ] coconut water – 3½ fl oz
- [ ] almonds (or other nut for nut milk) – 10½ oz
- [ ] pistachio nuts – ¼ oz
- [ ] cashew nuts – 2½ oz
- [ ] raisins
- [ ] walnuts
- [ ] flaked almonds
- [ ] pepitas (pumpkin seeds)
- [ ] sunflower seeds
- [ ] chia seeds
- [ ] toasted sesame seeds
- [ ] ground flaxseeds
- [ ] red lentils – 8 oz
- [ ] chickpeas – 5½ oz tinned
- [ ] brown rice – 1lb 1 oz
- [ ] quinoa – 7½ oz
- [ ] spaghetti – 2 oz
- [ ] finely shredded coconut
- [ ] sundried tomatoes
- [ ] za'atar
- [ ] cinnamon
- [ ] sumac
- [ ] paprika
- [ ] curry powder
- [ ] salt and pepper
- [ ] chili flakes
- [ ] olive oil
- [ ] grapeseed oil
- [ ] vegetable oil
- [ ] coconut oil
- [ ] toasted sesame oil
- [ ] balsamic vinegar
- [ ] malt vinegar
- [ ] rice vinegar
- [ ] all-purpose flour
- [ ] self-rising flour
- [ ] sesame flour
- [ ] chickpea flour (besan)
- [ ] cornstarch
- [ ] baking soda
- [ ] baking powder
- [ ] tahini
- [ ] soy sauce
- [ ] mirin
- [ ] white miso paste
- [ ] maple syrup
- [ ] raw (demerara) sugar
- [ ] coconut sugar
- [ ] sweet chili sauce
- [ ] agave syrup
- [ ] vanilla bean – 1
- [ ] natural vanilla extract
- [ ] rice paper rounds
- [ ] sourdough bread – 1 loaf, 3 slices
- [ ] panko breadcrumbs – 3½ oz
- [ ] nutritional yeast flakes

WEEK 1 PREP

Check to see if you have any of these items already made and if not, add ingredients to your shopping list.

BASICS
(these are items that you should have pre-prepped as they will last a while)
- [ ] Nut milk (p.8)
- [ ] Carrot & parsnip loaf (p.34)
- [ ] Garlic whip (p.26)
- [ ] Crunchy seed mix (p.24)
- [ ] Peanut butter (p.8)
- [ ] Vegan broth (p.30)
- [ ] Pesto (p.26)
- [ ] Tomato & chili relish (p.22)
- [ ] Tofu miso dressing (p.18)

MAKE
- [ ] Quick flatbread DAY 1 (p.36)
- [ ] Blueberry chia pudding DAY 2 (p.60)
- [ ] Brown rice dressing DAY 1 (p.58)
- [ ] Satay dipping sauce DAY 2 (p.60)
- [ ] Roasted sumac chickpeas DAY 3 (p.24)
- [ ] Flaxseed egg DAY 4 (p.14)

COOK
- [ ] Brown rice 9 oz DAYS 1 & 3
- [ ] Boil beets DAY 3 (p.62)

ROAST
- [ ] Cashew nuts DAY 1 (p.58)
- [ ] Chickpeas DAY 3 (p.62)

WEEK 1 TIMETABLE

10AM
PREP and **BAKE**
- Carrot & parsnip loaf (cool, slice half and freeze, save 2 slices for DAY 3)

10.30AM
COOK
- brown rice for DAYS 1 & 3

11AM
Meanwhile
MAKE
- Brown rice dressing
- Satay dipping sauce
- Boil beets

12PM
PREPARE
- Chia pudding for DAY 2 (leave in fridge)

DAY 01

WEEK 1

MONDAY

With your preparation done you will have quick breakfast and lunch recipes ready to go today.

BREAKFAST
Almond milk & pistachio porridge

SERVES: 1
PREP / COOK TIME
5 minutes plus overnight soak / 5 minutes

1 ¾ oz rolled (porridge) oats
½ teaspoon ground cinnamon, plus extra for sprinkling
½ cup almond milk
¼ oz pistachio nuts, roughly chopped

01 Soak oats and cinnamon in half the almond milk and leave in fridge overnight. Transfer oats to a pan and add remaining almond milk then cook over medium heat, stirring gently as porridge thickens. Add a little water to adjust consistency if needed. Serve, topped with cinnamon and chopped pistachio nuts.

Nutrition per serving:
320 cals / 16.39g fat / 51.25g carbs / 13.43g protein

LUNCH
Brown rice herb salad

SERVES: 1
PREP / COOK TIME
15 minutes / 30 minutes

9 oz warm cooked brown rice
1 scallion, thinly sliced
½ small red bell pepper, diced
1 tablespoon raisins
¼ oz roughly chopped flat-leaf parsley
¼ oz roughly chopped mint
¼ oz cashew nuts, roasted and roughly chopped

Brown rice dressing:
3 tablespoons olive oil
3 teaspoons soy sauce
2 teaspoons lemon juice
½ garlic clove, crushed
1 teaspoon finely grated ginger
salt and pepper

01 For dressing combine all ingredients in a small jar. Shake well to combine. Meanwhile, in a mixing bowl, combine warm rice with scallion, capsicum, raisins and herbs. Mix through to combine and allow heat of rice to soften additions. Cool before dressing and topping with roasted cashew nuts. Make ahead for a quick lunch.

Nutrition per serving:
851 cals / 48.32g fat / 84.31g carbs / 14.92g protein

DINNER
Eggplant pizzette

SERVES: 1
PREP / COOK TIME
10 minutes / 15 minutes

1 small eggplant, cut into thin slices lengthways
2 tablespoons olive oil
1 tablespoon za'atar
2 Quick flatbreads (p.36)
4 tablespoons Garlic whip (p.26)
¼ oz baby spinach leaves

01 Heat a griddle pan over high heat. Brush the eggplant with oil and cook for 3–4 minutes on each side. Sprinkle with za'atar and cool. Top each flatbread with garlic whip, spinach and grilled eggplant. Sprinkle with any extra za'atar and drizzle with olive oil. Heat under broiler for 1–2 minutes to warm through and serve. Store leftovers in fridge for another day.

Nutrition per serving:
715 cals / 28.85g fat / 95.99g carbs / 20.16g protein

BROWN RICE HERB SALAD

ALMOND MILK & PISTACHIO PORRIDGE

EGGPLANT PIZZETTE

DAY 02

WEEK 1

TUESDAY

There are plenty of fresh vegetables to fill you up today. You can swap different fruit or flavors in the chia recipe for another day.

BREAKFAST
Blueberry chia pudding

SERVES: 1
PREP / SET TIME
10 minutes / 2 hours

1 ¾ fl oz coconut milk or any nut milk
1 vanilla bean, split and seeds scraped out
½ tablespoon maple syrup (optional)
1 tablespoon chia seeds
¼ oz fresh blueberries

01 Whisk coconut milk, 1 tablespoon water, vanilla seeds, maple syrup (if using) and chia seeds together in a bowl. Leave for 5 minutes, then whisk again to make sure chia seeds are evenly dispersed. Add half the berries and mix through to combine. Transfer to a small serving bowl or jar. Cover and chill for 2 hours, or until set. Top with remaining berries. Store in fridge for up to 4 days.

Nutrition per serving:
174 cals / 12.1g fat / 16.21g carbs / 2.9g protein

LUNCH
Rainbow rice paper rolls with satay sauce

MAKES: 8
PREP / COOK TIME
15 minutes / 0 minutes

3 ½ oz red cabbage, shredded
1 carrot, julienned
1 ¾ oz beansprouts
¾ oz cilantro leaves
8 rice paper rounds

Satay dipping sauce:
2 oz crunchy peanut butter
1 teaspoon light soy sauce
1 tablespoon sweet chili sauce
½ garlic clove, crushed
1 tablespoon finely diced red onion
1 teaspoon curry powder
1 tablespoon finely diced lemongrass stalk
⅓ cup coconut milk

01 Mix all sauce ingredients together and set aside. Combine vegetables, beansprouts and cilantro in a bowl. Soften a rice paper round in a bowl of warm water, then place on clean dish towel. Top with 2 tablespoons of vegetables. Roll up. Serve with sauce. Store leftovers in fridge.

Nutrition per serving:
440 cals / 16.44g fat / 66.52g carbs / 10.24g protein

DINNER
Sesame tofu stir-fry

SERVES: 1
PREP / COOK TIME
10 minutes / 10 minutes

½ tablespoon coconut oil
4 ½ oz extra firm tofu, pressed and diced
7 oz mixed chopped vegetables
¾ oz beansprouts
1 scallion, sliced, cilantro and ½ tablespoon toasted sesame seeds, to serve

Sauce:
1 tablespoon grated ginger
2 teaspoons toasted sesame oil
2 tablespoons soy sauce
1 tablespoon rice vinegar
½ tablespoon agave syrup
¼ teaspoon chili flakes (optional)
½ tablespoon cornstarch

01 Whisk sauce ingredients with 1 tablespoon water. Heat a frying pan, add oil and swirl to coat pan. Add tofu and cook until browned. Set aside. Add vegetables and stir-fry for 2 minutes. Add 2 tablespoons of sauce and fry for 2 minutes. Toss in remaining sauce and fry until thickened slightly. Add beansprouts and tofu and toss. Sprinkle with serving suggestions.

Nutrition per serving:
539 cals / 34.78g fat / 38.9g carbs / 26.83g protein

BLUEBERRY CHIA PUDDING

SESAME TOFU STIR-FRY

RAINBOW RICE PAPER ROLLS WITH SATAY SAUCE

DAY 03

WEEK 1

WEDNESDAY

You are making extra lentil dal tonight to use for the rissoles on Friday night, so just pop the leftovers in the fridge until then.

BREAKFAST
Carrot & parsnip loaf with cinnamon tahini spread

SERVES: 1
PREP / COOK TIME
5 minutes / 5 minutes

2 slices Carrot & parsnip bread (p.34)
sliced strawberries, to serve

Cinnamon tahini spread:
2 tablespoons tahini
1 tablespoon maple syrup
½ teaspoon ground cinnamon

01 Toast bread. Meanwhile, in a small bowl, combine spread ingredients. Spread over toasted bread, top with strawberries and serve warm.

Nutrition per serving:
667 cals / 29.73g fat / 73.17g carbs / 10.72g protein

LUNCH
Warm beet & walnut salad

SERVES: 1
PREP / COOK TIME
5 minutes / 30 minutes

2 beets
1 tablespoon olive oil
¼ oz walnuts
2 teaspoons balsamic vinegar
1 oz mixed baby spinach and arugula
1 tablespoon Crunchy seed mix (p.24)
1 dill sprig
3 chives, finely chopped
sea salt flakes

01 Place beets in a pan of boiling water and boil for 20–30 minutes until soft to pierce with a fork. Peel off skin while beets are cooling.

02 Preheat oven to 350°F. Lay beets on a lined baking tray and drizzle with half the oil and salt. Roast for 10–12 minutes until golden. On another tray, toast walnuts for 4–5 minutes. Drizzle with remaining oil and vinegar. Roughly chop walnuts and sprinkle over spinach and arugula along with seed mix. Combine spinach and arugula, dill and chives, then toss through beets.

Nutrition per serving:
303 cals / 24.02g fat / 18.5g carbs / 6.94g protein

DINNER
Red lentil dal

SERVES: 2 PLUS EXTRA FOR MAKING RISSOLES FRIDAY NIGHT
PREP / COOK TIME
15 minutes / 30 minutes

1½ tablespoons coconut oil
1 large carrot, grated
1 parsnip, grated
1 onion, grated
2 garlic cloves, finely chopped
¾ inch piece of ginger, peeled and finely grated
2 teaspoons mild curry powder
2 cups Vegan broth (p.30)
8 oz dried red lentils
3½ oz baby spinach leaves
1 French shallot, thinly sliced
4½ oz cooked brown rice
1 tablespoon Roasted sumac chickpeas (p.24)

01 Heat ½ tablespoon of oil in a pan and fry carrot, parsnip, onion, garlic and spices for 4–5 minutes. Add broth and lentils and boil. Reduce heat to low, cover and cook until lentils are tender. Set half aside. Fold spinach through remaining mix in pan. In another pan, heat remaining oil and fry shallot until golden brown. Drain. Serve dal with rice, shallot and chickpeas.

Nutrition per serving:
391 cals / 7.34g fat / 67.77g carbs / 17.06g protein

CARROT & PARSNIP LOAF WITH CINNAMON TAHINI SPREAD

WARM BEET & WALNUT SALAD

RED LENTIL DAL

DAY 04

WEEK 1

THURSDAY

These recipes are extra quick with a great protein boost from the tofu dinner. The breakfast pudding can be prepared the night before and baked in the morning.

BREAKFAST
Baked brown rice pudding with peaches

SERVES: 1
PREP / COOK TIME
15 minutes / 10 minutes

½ Flaxseed egg (p.14)
½ cup non-dairy milk
grated zest of ½ lemon
½ teaspoon ground cinnamon
½ teaspoon natural vanilla extract
3½ oz cooked brown rice
½ peach, sliced
½ tablespoon flaked almonds

01 Preheat oven to 350°F. Whisk flaxseed egg, milk, lemon zest, cinnamon and vanilla together in a bowl. Tip rice into a 1-cup ramekin, then pour liquid over rice. Layer top with peach slices and flaked almonds before baking. Bake for 10 minutes, or until set. Enjoy warm.

Nutrition per serving:
240 cals / 6.2g fat / 40.48g carbs / 6.41g protein

LUNCH
Avocado pesto toasts

SERVES: 1
PREP / COOK TIME
5 minutes / 5 minutes

½–1 avocado, flesh diced
2 tablespoons Pesto (p.26)
juice of ½ lemon
salt and pepper
2 slices sourdough bread
Crunchy seed mix (p.24)

01 In a small bowl, gently combine avocado, pesto, lemon juice and seasoning. Toast sourdough and top with avocado mix, then sprinkle with seed mix.

Nutrition per serving:
452 cals / 39.28g fat / 18.3g carbs / 13.08g protein

DINNER
Barbecued tofu with bok choy & broccolini

SERVES: 1
PREP / COOK TIME
40 minutes / 10 minutes

2 thick slices of extra firm tofu (5½–7 oz)
2 teaspoons sumac
1 teaspoon paprika
1 garlic clove, crushed
1 tablespoon olive oil, plus extra for cooking
2 tablespoons lemon juice
3 broccolini sprigs, blanched
1 head bok choy, halved
2 tablespoons Satay dipping sauce (p.60)

01 Make sure tofu has been pressed and drained of any excess water. In a small bowl, whisk sumac, paprika, garlic, oil and lemon juice together, then pour over tofu slices. Use your fingertips to rub into tofu. Leave for 30 minutes.

02 Heat griddle pan and brush with oil. Cook tofu on either side for 4–5 minutes until well colored and charred. When cooking last side, add broccolini, then bok choy and leave to soften and char slightly. Serve with satay sauce.

Nutrition per serving:
547 cals / 33.24g fat / 32.36g carbs / 46.18g protein

BAKED BROWN RICE PUDDING WITH PEACHES

AVOCADO PESTO TOASTS

BARBECUED TOFU WITH BOK CHOY & BROCCOLINI

DAY 05

WEEK 1

FRIDAY

Green smoothies are a great go-to breakfast, as they are so quick. You can add all types of greens – kale, spinach, bok choy and lettuce all work well.

BREAKFAST
Best green smoothie

SERVES: 1
PREP / COOK TIME
5 minutes / 0 minutes

1 oz baby spinach leaves
½ frozen banana
3½ oz frozen mango
2 heaped spoonfuls coconut yogurt
3½ fl oz coconut water

01 Add all ingredients to a blender and blend until smooth. Add more water or coconut water if needed to achieve desired consistency.

Nutrition per serving:
267 cals / 7.99g fat / 51.29g carbs / 3.61g protein

LUNCH
Quinoa tabbouleh

SERVES: 1
PREP / COOK TIME
20 minutes / 12 minutes

3 oz quinoa
1 bunch of mixed herbs, (flat-leaf parsley, cilantro, mint), finely chopped
½ small red onion, finely diced
2 roma (plum) tomatoes, finely diced
½ small Persian cucumber, diced
juice of ½ lemon
1 tablespoon olive oil
sea salt

01 Rinse and drain quinoa, then combine with 1 cup water in a small pan. Bring to the boil, cover and reduce heat. Simmer for 10–12 minutes. Stir, remove from heat and leave, covered, for 10 minutes.

02 Mix quinoa, herbs, onion, tomatoes and cucumber together, then pour lemon juice and olive oil over. Toss and season before serving.

Nutrition per serving:
304 cals / 16.02g fat / 35.96g carbs / 7.4g protein

DINNER
Lentil rissoles with tomato & chili relish & cucumber raita

SERVES: 1
PREP / COOK TIME
15 minutes / 20 minutes

left-over Red lentil dal (p.62)
3½ oz panko breadcrumbs
salt and pepper
Tomato & chili relish (p.22), to serve

Cucumber raita:
¼ cup coconut or other vegan yogurt
¼ Persian cucumber, finely diced
1 tablespoon finely shredded mint
sea salt and pepper

01 Preheat oven to 350°F. Mix lentil dal and breadcrumbs together, then roll into balls or patties and set on a lined baking tray. Season and bake in oven for 15–20 minutes until crisp and golden on outside.

02 Meanwhile, mix raita ingredients together. Serve rissoles with raita and the relish. Freeze left-over rissoles for another time, then reheat.

Nutrition per serving:
549 cals / 22.39g fat / 74.28g carbs / 18.94g protein

QUINOA TABBOULEH

BEST GREEN SMOOTHIE

LENTIL RISSOLES WITH TOMATO & CHILI RELISH & CUCUMBER RAITA

DAY 06

WEEK 1

SATURDAY

Weekend days mean a little more time for a slow breakfast cook-up. Feel free to add more vegetables into the scramble if you have lots of leftovers from the week.

BREAKFAST
Tofu scramble

SERVES: 1
PREP / COOK TIME
5 minutes / 10 minutes

1 tablespoon olive oil
1 scallion, finely diced
½ red bell pepper, cut into strips
1 roma (plum) tomato, diced
5½ oz crumbled tofu (extra firm pressed, then crumbled)
salt and pepper
6 basil leaves, shredded
1 tablespoon chopped flat-leaf parsley
2 handfuls of baby spinach leaves
sweet chili sauce, to serve (optional)

01 Heat oil in a frying pan and fry scallion, pepper, tomato and tofu for 5–6 minutes. Season and mix through herbs and spinach. Toss together over heat until spinach has wilted slightly. Serve with extra seasoning as needed and sweet chili sauce, if liked.

Nutrition per serving:
383 cals / 27.14g fat / 16.74g carbs / 26.25g protein

LUNCH
Tomato salad with garlic croutons

SERVES: 1
PREP / COOK TIME
10 minutes / 6 minutes

2 tablespoons olive oil
1 slice of sourdough bread, cut into cubes
2 garlic cloves, crushed
1 handful of mixed heirloom tomatoes, sliced
¼ ruby red grapefruit, flesh segmented
¼ oz basil and mint leaves, shredded
sea salt and pepper

01 Preheat oven to 350°F. Pour half the oil over sourdough in a bowl, then add garlic and toss to coat. Spread bread cubes out evenly on a lined baking tray and cook for 5–6 minutes until golden and crisp.

02 Meanwhile, toss remaining ingredients together, drizzle with remaining oil and season well. Serve with crunchy croutons on top.

Nutrition per serving:
316 cals / 30.7g fat / 81.6g carbs / 16.72g protein

DINNER
Stuffed portobello mushrooms

SERVES: 1
PREP / COOK TIME
10 minutes / 25 minutes

½ small sweet potato, peeled and diced
1 garlic clove
1 rosemary sprig
2 large portobello mushrooms, stalks removed
2 tablespoons olive oil
sea salt
4½ oz cooked quinoa (see p.66)
1 tablespoon Crunchy seed mix (p.24)
1 tablespoon chopped sundried tomatoes
1 tablespoon nutritional yeast flakes
2 tablespoons Pesto (p.26)

01 Preheat oven to 350°F. Place sweet potato, garlic, rosemary and mushrooms on a lined baking tray. Drizzle with half the oil, sprinkle with salt and roast for 12–15 minutes until golden. Combine quinoa, sweet potato, garlic, rosemary leaves, seed mix, tomatoes and yeast flakes. Toss together with remaining oil. Season. Use the mix to stuff mushrooms. Add a tablespoon of pesto to each mushroom and heat for 5–10 minutes.

Nutrition per serving:
660 cals / 32.7g fat / 41.96g carbs / 16.37g protein

TOFU SCRAMBLE

TOMATO SALAD WITH GARLIC CROUTONS

STUFFED PORTOBELLO MUSHROOMS

DAY 07

WEEK 1
SUNDAY

These breakfast hash browns are an excellent Sunday treat. This recipe makes extra, so store them in the fridge for snacking later.

BREAKFAST

Hash browns with spinach & avocado

SERVES: 1
PREP / COOK TIME
15 minutes / 15 minutes

½ sweet potato, peeled and grated
2 russet potatoes, peeled and grated
1 tablespoon chickpea flour (besan)
sea salt and pepper
coconut or vegetable oil, for shallow-frying
finely chopped herbs, if some left over from the week
¾ oz baby spinach leaves
½ avocado, halved, pitted and sliced
1 lemon wedge, to serve

01 Combine grated potatoes in a colander and press down to drain excess liquid. Transfer to a bowl, add flour and season. Heat enough oil for shallow-frying in a frying pan over medium–high heat. Use your hands to portion a ball of potato mix and squeeze again to form a round ball. Drop 2–3 into hot oil and flatten with a spatula. Cook on each side for 3–4 minutes until crispy. Flip over to cook other side, then cool on paper towel. Steam spinach for 1–2 minutes. Serve with hash browns, sliced avocado and lemon.

Nutrition per serving:
579.5 cals / 69.66g fat / 84.19g carbs / 11.64g protein

LUNCH

Butter lettuce miso salad

SERVES: 1
PREP / COOK TIME
15 minutes / 0 minutes

¼ head of butter lettuce, leaves torn
2 small French breakfast radishes, thinly sliced
½ sweetcorn cob, kernels cut off
1 scallion, thinly sliced
1 flat-leaf parsley sprig, leaves chopped
1–2 tablespoons Tofu miso dressing (p.18)

01 Combine all ingredients in a bowl and toss to combine. Serve.

Nutrition per serving:
350 cals / 4.22g fat / 73.97g carbs / 13.46g protein

DINNER

Fresh pesto pasta

SERVES: 1
PREP / COOK TIME
5 minutes / 10 minutes

2 oz spaghetti or pasta of choice
pinch of salt
2 tablespoons Pesto (p.26)
½ tablespoon oil
½ tablespoon nutritional yeast flakes (optional)

01 Cook spaghetti in a pan of salted boiling water according to packet instructions. Once pasta is cooked, drain through a colander, reserving about 1 tablespoon of cooking water. Add pesto, oil and yeast, if using, to pan and heat over medium heat. Add cooked pasta, stir to combine and heat through. Season and serve.

Nutrition per serving:
343 cals / 25.04g fat / 21.63g carbs / 8.76g protein

HASH BROWNS WITH SPINACH & AVOCADO

BUTTER LETTUCE MISO SALAD

FRESH PESTO PASTA

WEEK TWO
WEEKLY SHOPPING LIST

FRUIT & VEG
- [ ] cilantro – 2 bunches
- [ ] mint – 1 bunch
- [ ] flat-leaf parsley – 3 bunches
- [ ] dill
- [ ] red onion – 2 small
- [ ] onions – 2 small
- [ ] French shallot – 1
- [ ] shiitake mushrooms – 5
- [ ] ginger – ¾ inch piece
- [ ] garlic – 1 bulb + 8 cloves
- [ ] curly kale – 1 bunch
- [ ] cavolo nero – 1 bunch
- [ ] green beans – 2¾ oz
- [ ] enoki mushroom – 1
- [ ] oyster mushrooms – 1 oz
- [ ] scallions – 7
- [ ] French breakfast radish – 1
- [ ] cauliflower – ¼
- [ ] sweet potato – 1
- [ ] baby spinach leaves – 1 oz
- [ ] mixed sprouts
- [ ] snow peas – 1½ oz
- [ ] snow pea shoots – 4½ oz
- [ ] arugula – ¾ oz
- [ ] watercress – 1¾ oz
- [ ] pear – 1
- [ ] strawberries – 6
- [ ] lemons – 3
- [ ] limes – 2
- [ ] cucumbers – 2
- [ ] red chilies – 2
- [ ] red cabbage – ¼
- [ ] white cabbage – 14 oz
- [ ] iceberg lettuce
- [ ] avocados – 2
- [ ] fennel bulb – 1
- [ ] orange – 1
- [ ] red apple – 1
- [ ] baby carrots – 1 bunch
- [ ] carrot – 1
- [ ] blueberries – 4½ oz (8–10)
- [ ] eggplant – 1
- [ ] roma (plum) tomatoes – 3
- [ ] jalapeño – 1

- [ ] stone fruit – 3
- [ ] bananas – 2
- [ ] bok choy – 2 heads
- [ ] broccolini – 1 bunch
- [ ] butternut squash – 1
- [ ] red bell pepper – 1
- [ ] edamame (fresh soy beans), podded – 1 oz

CHILLED/FROZEN
- [ ] soy milk
- [ ] almond or oat milk (or make, p.8) – 1 cup
- [ ] coconut yogurt – 4½ oz
- [ ] frozen mango pieces – 5½ oz

CHECK TO SEE IF IN PANTRY
- [ ] gyoza wrappers – 10
- [ ] silken tofu – 2 oz
- [ ] white miso paste
- [ ] diced tomatoes – 14 oz tinned
- [ ] cannellini beans – 21 oz tinned
- [ ] black beans – 7 oz tinned
- [ ] chickpeas – 14 oz tinned
- [ ] Puy lentils – 3½ oz
- [ ] rolled (porridge) oats
- [ ] soba noodles – 1¼ oz
- [ ] thick rice noodles – 3½ oz
- [ ] water chestnuts – 1 tin
- [ ] coconut cream – 14 oz tinned
- [ ] marinated artichoke hearts – 2 oz
- [ ] flaked almonds
- [ ] ground almonds
- [ ] pine nuts
- [ ] coconut flakes
- [ ] pecans
- [ ] dried cherries
- [ ] chia seeds
- [ ] sunflower seeds
- [ ] poppy seeds
- [ ] sesame seeds
- [ ] ground flaxseeds
- [ ] smoked paprika
- [ ] ground cumin
- [ ] chili powder
- [ ] ground turmeric

- [ ] ground ginger
- [ ] ground cinnamon
- [ ] sumac
- [ ] sea salt and black pepper
- [ ] finely shredded coconut
- [ ] wakame (dried seaweed)
- [ ] dijon mustard
- [ ] maple syrup
- [ ] tahini
- [ ] vegan Thai red curry paste
- [ ] all-purpose flour
- [ ] sesame flour
- [ ] chickpea flour (besan)
- [ ] coconut flour
- [ ] protein powder
- [ ] raw (demerara) sugar
- [ ] baking powder
- [ ] vanilla protein powder
- [ ] tamari
- [ ] rice wine vinegar
- [ ] apple cider vinegar
- [ ] mirin
- [ ] vegetable oil
- [ ] coconut oil
- [ ] olive oil
- [ ] toasted sesame oil
- [ ] red wine vinegar
- [ ] pumpernickel bread – 4 slices minimum
- [ ] nutritional yeast flakes
- [ ] kimchi
- [ ] crusty bread
- [ ] natural vanilla extract
- [ ] self-rising flour
- [ ] coconut sugar
- [ ] black sesame seeds
- [ ] cashew nuts
- [ ] quinoa
- [ ] hot chili sauce
- [ ] dried chickpeas
- [ ] coconut water

WEEK 2 PREP

Check to see if you have any of these items already made and if not, add ingredients to your shopping list.

BASICS
(these are items that you should have pre-prepped as they will last a while)
- [ ] Tofu cream cheese (p.26)
- [ ] Red wine vinaigrette (p.16)
- [ ] Beet hummus (p.40)
- [ ] Sauerkraut (p.20)
- [ ] Pesto (p.26)
- [ ] Tomato & chili relish (p.22)
- [ ] Pico de gallo (p.28)
- [ ] Granola (p.32)
- [ ] Vegan broth (p.30)
- [ ] Vegan aïoli (p.18)
- [ ] Crunch seed mix (p.24)

PREP
- [ ] Soak chickpeas Day 10 (p.78)

MAKE
- [ ] Flaxseed or Chia seed egg DAY 9 (p.14)
- [ ] Coconut yogurt lime chili dressing DAY 9 (p.18)
- [ ] Chargrilled eggplant & sumac dip DAY 10 (p.40)
- [ ] Quick flatbread DAY 12 (p.36)
- [ ] Chickpea flour crêpes DAY 13 (p.36)

COOK
- [ ] Quinoa – 1 lb 5 oz uncooked (6½ oz cooked)

WEEK 2 TIMETABLE

10AM
PREP and **Bake**
- Sweet potato muffins (DAY 9). When cool, freeze extras for snacks.

10.30AM
MAKE
- Bean shakshuka (DAYS 8 & 9)
COOK
- quinoa (DAY 9)

11AM
Meanwhile
MAKE
- Chargrilled eggplant & sumac dip (DAY 10)
- Beet hummus (DAY 10)

12PM
MAKE
- Falafel mix (DAY 10)
- Coconut yogurt, lime, chili dressing (DAY 9)

DAY 08

WEEK 2
MONDAY

Prepare this delicious breakfast the night before so all you need to do is reheat it in the morning. You can also make extra and mix into a weeknight dinner.

Bean shakshuka with cilantro

SERVES: 2
PREP / COOK TIME
10 minutes / 15 minutes

1 tablespoon olive oil
1 small red onion, finely diced
2 garlic cloves, crushed
2 teaspoons smoked paprika
1 teaspoon ground cumin
1 teaspoon chili powder
3 kale stalks, leaves removed and chopped
14 oz tinned diced tomatoes
14 oz tinned cannellini beans
7 oz tinned black beans
2 tablespoons Tofu cream cheese (p.26)
¼ oz cilantro leaves, chopped
salt and pepper
crusty bread, to serve

01 Warm oil in a large pan over medium heat and fry onion and garlic for a few minutes. Add spices and kale and fry until kale has wilted slightly. Pour in tomatoes and beans and simmer for 5–6 minutes. Top with dollop of tofu cream cheese and cilantro. Season to taste. Serve with crusty bread.

Nutrition per serving:
543 cals / 13.41g fat / 83.51g carbs / 27.97g protein

Miso soup with kimchi

SERVES: 1
PREP / COOK TIME
5 minutes / 15 minutes

¼ oz wakame (dried seaweed)
1 heaped tablespoon kimchi
½ oz white miso paste
1 scallion, sliced, to serve

01 Bring 1 cup water to the boil in a medium pan. Reduce heat to a simmer, add wakame and kimchi and heat through. Remove a few spoonfuls of cooking water and mix in a small cup with miso to soften. Whisk miso into pan and simmer gently while stirring to combine.

02 Divide among serving bowls and top with sliced scallion.

Nutrition per serving:
38 cals / 1.05g fat / 5.54g carbs / 2.31g protein

Roasted cauliflower salad

SERVES: 1
PREP / COOK TIME
10 minutes / 20 minutes

½ red onion, cut into wedges
7 oz sweet potato, diced
¼ cauliflower, cut into small florets
½ tablespoon olive oil
sea salt and pepper
2 tablespoons pine nuts
1¾ oz mixed baby spinach and arugula leaves
2 tablespoons Red wine vinaigrette (p.16)

01 Preheat oven to 375°F. Combine red onion, sweet potato and cauliflower on a large baking tray. Drizzle with oil and season well. Roast for 15–20 minutes until edges of vegetables are starting to caramelize. Spread pine nuts out on another baking tray and toast for the last 5 minutes of cooking.

02 Toss all ingredients together to combine.

Nutrition per serving:
631 cals / 46.24g fat / 49.19g carbs / 10.23g protein

BEAN SHAKSHUKA WITH CILANTRO

MISO SOUP WITH KIMCHI

ROASTED CAULIFLOWER SALAD

DAY 09

WEEK 2
TUESDAY

These muffins will keep for up to 4 days in an airtight container or can be frozen individually and saved for a quick breakfast or instant snack.

Sweet potato muffins

MAKES: 6 SMALL MUFFINS
PREP / COOK TIME
10 minutes / 30 minutes

2 Flaxseed or Chia seed eggs (p.14)
2 oz silken tofu
3 tablespoons maple syrup
1 teaspoon natural vanilla extract
4½ oz wholewheat self-rising flour
1 oz ground almonds
1¾ oz coconut sugar or an alternative
½ teaspoon baking powder
½ teaspoon ground ginger
1 teaspoon ground cinnamon
5½ oz sweet potato, grated
1 pear, finely diced
oil, for oiling
3 tablespoons Granola (p.32)

01 Preheat oven to 340°F. Prepare flaxseed or chia egg. Whisk tofu, maple syrup and vanilla together. In another bowl, combine flour, almonds, sugar, baking powder and spices. Make a well in center and fold in tofu and flaxseed egg. Mix in potato and pear. Divide between an oiled 6-hole muffin tin and top with granola. Bake for 25–30 minutes until golden brown. Cool in tin for 5 minutes, then transfer to a wire rack to cool.

Nutrition per serving:
251 cals / 6.88g fat / 43.77g carbs / 6.57g protein

Mixed sprout salad

SERVES: 1
PREP / COOK TIME
10 minutes / 0 minutes

1 oz mixed sprouts (mung, chickpea, salad sprouts) (p.10)
¼ oz snow pea shoots
½ oz beansprouts
¼ oz mint, chopped
½ Persian cucumber, thinly sliced
1 teaspoon black sesame seeds
½ red chili, thinly sliced (optional)
1–2 tablespoons Coconut yogurt lime chili dressing (p.18)
¾ oz chopped roasted cashew nuts

01 Combine all ingredients, except cashew nuts, in a bowl and toss together. Top salad with cashew nuts and serve.

Nutrition per serving:
246 cals / 9.66g fat / 21.17g carbs / 6.94g protein

Quinoa Mex bowl

SERVES: 1
PREP / COOK TIME
10 minutes / 5 minutes

1 oz quinoa uncooked or 3 oz cooked
7 oz precooked Bean shakshuka, (p.74)
1 oz red cabbage, shredded
1 oz iceberg lettuce, shredded
1 tablespoon Pico de gallo (p.28)
¼ oz cilantro leaves
½ avocado, sliced
hot chili sauce, to taste

01 If cooking quinoa, bring quinoa and 5½ fl oz water to the boil in a pan, then reduce heat to simmer. Cover with a lid and cook for 10–12 minutes until all water has absorbed. Turn off heat and let quinoa stand, covered, in pan for another 10 minutes before stirring with a fork to fluff.

02 If using precooked quinoa, then heat in a pan with bean shakshuka. Layer all ingredients into a serving bowl.

Nutrition per serving:
1137 cals / 46.74g fat / 152.35g carbs / 42.19g protein

SWEET POTATO MUFFINS

MIXED SPROUT SALAD

QUINOA MEX BOWL

DAY 10

WEEK 2
WEDNESDAY

Think ahead and have this bircher made and in the fridge on Tuesday night, then you can just add the berries, yogurt and apple for a quick breakfast.

Bircher muesli

SERVES: 1
PREP / SOAK TIME
5 minutes / at least 1 hour or overnight

1 tablespoon chia seeds
1 tablespoon vanilla protein powder
2 tablespoons rolled (porridge) oats
juice of 1 orange
1 heaped tablespoon plant-based yogurt
8–10 blueberries
¼ red apple, cored and julienned

01 In a small bowl, mix together chia seeds, protein powder, oats and orange juice. Cover and refrigerate overnight (it can be just an hour if you forget).

02 Serve muesli with yogurt, berries and apple on top.

Nutrition per serving:
225 cals / 7.63g fat / 36.95g carbs / 29.12g protein

Pumpernickel with hummus & cucumber

SERVES: 1
PREP / COOK TIME
5 minutes / 5 minutes

2 slices of pumpernickel bread
2 oz hummus or Beet hummus (p.40)
½ Persian cucumber, sliced
salt and pepper
lemon wedge, to serve

01 Toast pumpernickel to your taste. Layer with hummus and sliced cucumber, then season and serve with a lemon wedge to squeeze.

Nutrition per serving:
449 cals / 26.1g fat / 44.98g carbs / 15.78g protein

Falafel plate

SERVES: 1 (MAKES 9–10 FALAFEL)
PREP / COOK TIME
40 minutes / 10 minutes

4½ oz dried chickpeas, soaked overnight
4 scallions
2 garlic cloves
1 bunch of flat-leaf parsley
1 bunch of cilantro
½ bunch of mint
1 tablespoon sesame seeds
½ teaspoon ground cumin
¼ teaspoon ground black pepper
½ teaspoon baking powder
sea salt
2 cups vegetable oil, for frying
lettuce, tomato, Sauerkraut (p.20), flat-leaf parsley, Chargrilled eggplant & sumac dip (p.40) and olive oil, to serve

01 Blitz all ingredients, except oil and serving suggestions, with 1 teaspoon salt in a food processor until finely chopped. Cover and chill for 30 minutes. Heat oil in a deep pan to 350°F. Press 1½ tablespoons of mixture to make a round patty and deep-fry in hot oil for 3–4 minutes. Fry in 2–3 batches. Remove and season with salt. Serve with accompaniments. Freeze leftovers for later.

Nutrition per serving:
263 cals / 9.8g fat / 35.91g carbs / 18.65g protein

BIRCHER MUESLI

PUMPERNICKEL WITH HUMMUS & CUCUMBER

FALAFEL PLATE

DAY 11

WEEK 2
THURSDAY

You could make a double batch of the gyoza and freeze some for next time – planning saves so much time in the long run.

Roasted stone fruit crumble

SERVES: 2
PREP / COOK TIME
10 minutes / 30 minutes

¾ oz pecans, roughly chopped
¾ oz coconut flour
1 tablespoon finely shredded coconut
¾ oz coconut oil (preferably solid)
selection of 3 ripe stone fruits (peach, plum, apricot), cut into small wedges
½ teaspoon ground cinnamon
½ tablespoon maple syrup (optional)

01 Preheat oven to 400°F. Combine pecans with flour and coconut. Roughly rub coconut oil into flour mix with your fingertips. Set aside in fridge.

02 Place fruit wedges on a baking tray. Sprinkle with cinnamon and drizzle with maple syrup, if using, and roast for 20 minutes, or until softened.

03 Divide fruit between 2 small ramekins. Spoon 2 tablespoons of flour mix on top of each ramekin and bake for 10 minutes until golden brown. Freeze other portion for another time.

Nutrition per serving:
317 cals / 27.29g fat / 20.46g carbs / 4.66g protein

Simple kale salad

SERVES: 1
PREP / COOK TIME
10 minutes / 0 minutes

1 curly green kale stalk
1 cavolo nero stalk
1½ tablespoons olive oil
6–8 green beans
½ Persian cucumber
1 mint sprig
1 tablespoon Crunchy seed mix (p.24)
juice of ½ lime
1 handful of pea shoots
salt and pepper
lime wedge, to serve

01 Remove leaves from kale and cavolo nero stalks and cut into fine ribbons. Place in a bowl and rub 1 tablespoon of oil into leaves. Leave while preparing remaining ingredients.

02 Chop green beans, cucumber and mint. Combine with kale, then sprinkle seed mix over salad. Dress with lime juice and remaining oil. Top with pea shoots and season. Serve with lime.

Nutrition per serving:
589 cals / 49.09g fat / 26.57g carbs / 1.17g protein

Vegetable gyoza with bok choy

MAKES: 10
PREP / COOK TIME
20 minutes / 5 minutes

2 heads bok choy, halved lengthways
6 water chestnuts, finely diced
1 scallion, thinly sliced
1 shiitake mushroom, finely diced
¼ oz piece of ginger, peeled and grated
2 teaspoons tamari
½ teaspoon toasted sesame oil
10 gyoza wrappers
2 teaspoons vegetable oil, for frying

01 Finely chop half of one bok choy head. Mix with remaining ingredients, except wrappers and oil, in a bowl. Lay 1 wrapper on a damp dish towel, place 1 teaspoon of mix in center of wrapper, brush outside of wrapper with water and fold and crimp outer edges together. Repeat with remaining wrappers. Heat oil in a frying pan and cook gyoza on one side until crispy and browned. Add 3 tablespoons water and cover. Leave for 3–4 minutes until transparent. Add remaining bok choy and steam for a few minutes. Serve. Set leftovers aside for another time.

Nutrition per serving:
554 cals / 8.29g fat / 99.98g carbs / 17.44g protein

ROASTED STONE FRUIT CRUMBLE

SIMPLE KALE SALAD

VEGETABLE GYOZA WITH BOK CHOY

DAY 12

WEEK 2
FRIDAY

Use a coconut yogurt to make the flatbreads – they will have a sweet coconut flavor, which is delicious with this roasted vegetable soup.

Kale & mixed mushroom toasts

SERVES: 1
PREP / COOK TIME
5 minutes / 10 minutes

1 tablespoon coconut oil
1 garlic clove, thinly sliced
2 oz mixed mushrooms, enoki, oyster and button, sliced
1 curly kale or cavolo nero stalk, leaves removed and chopped
1 teaspoon tamari
2 slices pumpernickel or other bread
1 tablespoon hot chili sauce or chutney (use Pesto, p.26 or Tomato & chili relish, p.22 left over from week 1)

01 Heat oil in a small pan and fry garlic and mushrooms for 3–4 minutes. Add kale and tamari and fry until kale softens and wilts.

02 Toast bread and spread with chili sauce or your choice of spread. Heap with kale and mushroom mixture and serve.

Nutrition per serving:
331 cals / 15.37g fat / 46.23g carbs / 8.39g protein

Cold soba noodle salad

SERVES: 1
PREP / COOK TIME
10 minutes / 15 minutes

1¼ oz buckwheat soba noodles
½ bunch of broccolini
1 oz podded edamame (fresh soy beans)
1 French breakfast radish, thinly sliced
1 scallion, sliced

Dressing:
1 tablespoon tamari
1 tablespoon rice wine vinegar
1 teaspoon mirin
½ tablespoon toasted sesame oil
½ red chili, finely diced (optional)

01 Bring a large pot of water to the boil and cook soba noodles according to packet instructions. In last few minutes of cooking, add broccolini. Drain and rinse noodles and broccolini in cold water. Mix all dressing ingredients together in a jar. Combine cooked noodles and broccolini in a bowl with edamame, radish and scallion. Pour dressing over and mix together.

Nutrition per serving:
308 cals / 8.22g fat / 48.59g carbs / 14.12g protein

Roasted squash & carrot soup

SERVES: 2
PREP / COOK TIME
15 minutes / 30 minutes

10½ oz butternut squash, peeled and cut into chunks
1 bunch of baby carrots (5–6)
1 garlic clove
1 small onion, quartered
½ tablespoon olive oil
salt and pepper
12 fl oz Vegan broth (p.30) or water
½ Quick flatbread (p.36)
½ teaspoon ground turmeric
1 teaspoon ground cumin
1 tablespoon chopped flat-leaf parsley, to serve

01 Preheat oven to 375°F. Combine squash, carrots, garlic and onion. Drizzle with oil and season. Roast for 20–25 minutes, stirring halfway through. Bring broth to the boil in a pan. Blitz flatbread in a food processor until crumbs. Blend slightly cooled vegetables, spices and half the broth in a blender, slowly adding remaining broth until desired consistency. Season. Serve with parsley and breadcrumbs. Freeze other portion.

Nutrition per serving:
727 cals / 12.36g fat / 135.45g carbs / 21.99g protein

KALE & MIXED MUSHROOM TOASTS

COLD SOBA NOODLE SALAD

ROASTED SQUASH & CARROT SOUP

DAY 13

WEEK 2
SATURDAY

Start to look through the fridge and use any extra produce on the crêpe, or add it to the lentil salad today.

Mango smoothie bowl

SERVES: 1
PREP / COOK TIME
5 minutes / 0 minutes

5½ oz frozen mango pieces
½ frozen banana
1 tablespoon vanilla protein powder
¼ cup coconut yogurt
1 tablespoon maple syrup
¼ cup coconut water
½ banana, sliced
2 tablespoons Granola (p.32)
1 tablespoon toasted coconut flakes

01 Blend mango, frozen banana, protein powder, coconut yogurt and maple syrup together in a blender until smooth. Add coconut water and continue to blend. Depending on preferred consistency you may like to reduce or increase amount of coconut water. Serve in a bowl, topped with sliced banana, granola and coconut flakes.

Nutrition per serving:
415 cals / 13.66g fat / 72.82g carbs / 25.52g protein

Avocado & sauerkraut chickpea crêpe

SERVES: 1
PREP / COOK TIME
10 minutes / 10 minutes

2 Chickpea flour crêpes (p.36)
1 avocado, peeled, pitted and sliced
1 roma (plum) tomato, sliced
salt and pepper
4 tablespoons Sauerkraut (p.20)
lime wedge, to serve

01 Cook the crêpes according to instructions on p.36. Layer avocado and tomato onto crêpe and season. Top with sauerkraut before folding crêpe over and serving with lime.

Nutrition per serving:
415 cals / 36.48g fat / 23.72g carbs / 6.06g protein

Warm lentil watercress salad

SERVES: 2
PREP / COOK TIME
10 minutes / 35 minutes

2 tablespoons olive oil
1 small onion, finely diced
2 garlic cloves, finely chopped
1 teaspoon ground cumin
1 small carrot, diced
1 large roma (plum) tomato, diced
3½ oz Puy lentils
5 fl oz Vegan broth (p.30) or water
sea salt and pepper
1 teaspoon red wine vinegar
2 tablespoons finely chopped cilantro
1¾ oz watercress

01 Heat half the oil in a heavy pan and gently fry onion for 10 minutes. Add garlic and cumin and fry for 2 minutes, then add carrot, tomato, lentils and broth and bring to the boil. Reduce heat to a simmer, season and cook, covered, for 25 minutes. Stir in vinegar, rest of oil and cilantro. Cover and cool slightly. Fold through watercress and season. Set leftovers aside in fridge for another time.

Nutrition per serving:
351 cals / 14.59g fat / 43.45g carbs / 14.71g protein

MANGO SMOOTHIE BOWL

AVOCADO & SAUERKRAUT CHICKPEA CRÊPE

WARM LENTIL WATERCRESS SALAD

DAY 14

WEEK 2
SUNDAY

Extra greens will go well in both the lunch and dinner today, so bulk up the meal with more vegetables and flavor if you have them.

BREAKFAST
Banana pancakes

MAKES: 10
PREP / COOK TIME
10 minutes / 10 minutes

1 large overripe banana, mashed
1 tablespoon coconut oil melted, plus extra for cooking
1 tablespoon vanilla protein powder
2 teaspoons baking powder
7½ fl oz–1 cup almond milk (p.8)
8 oz all-purpose flour
1 oz ground almonds
banana and strawberry slices and maple syrup, to serve

01 Whisk banana, oil, protein powder, baking powder and 7½ fl oz almond milk together until combined well. Add flour and ground almonds and gently stir until smooth. Mix shouldn't be too thick, so add more milk if needed.

02 Heat a large nonstick frying pan, oil pan and spoon ¼ cup of batter into pan. Cook 2–3 pancakes at once for 2–3 minutes until bubbles form on top. Flip and cook other side. Repeat with remaining batter. Serve with fruit and maple syrup. Chill leftovers for another time.

Nutrition per serving:
321 cals / 11.62g fat / 47.14g carbs / 29.13g protein

LUNCH
Quick white bean salad

SERVES: 1
PREP / COOK TIME
10 minutes / 0 minutes

1–2 tablespoons Vegan aïoli (p.18)
juice of ½ lemon
7 oz tinned cannellini beans, drained and rinsed
½ small red onion, finely diced
1 oz flat-leaf parsley, leaves finely chopped
½ red bell pepper, chopped
2 oz marinated artichoke hearts, chopped
salt and pepper
lemon wedge, to serve

01 In a small bowl, combine aïoli, lemon juice and season to taste. Set aside.

02 Mix remaining ingredients together in a medium bowl. Add dressing and stir through to coat. Serve with lemon wedge.

Nutrition per serving:
468 cals / 17.5g fat / 65.05g carbs / 18.03g protein

DINNER
Coconut noodle soup with chili & lime

SERVES: 1
PREP / COOK TIME
5 minutes / 15 minutes

½ tablespoon coconut oil
1 teaspoon finely chopped ginger
1 French shallot, finely diced
1 red chili, seeded and finely diced, plus extra to garnish
1 tablespoon vegan Thai red curry paste
1 cup coconut cream
1 cup Vegan broth (p.30) or water
3½ oz thick rice noodles
1½ oz snow peas
juice of 1 lime, plus wedges to serve
¼ oz cilantro leaves, to garnish

01 Heat oil in a pan over medium–high heat and fry ginger, shallot, chili and curry paste for a few minutes until fragrant. Add coconut cream and broth and bring to the boil. Reduce heat to a simmer. Add noodles and cook for 4–5 minutes until tender. Remove from heat and add snow peas and lime juice. Garnish with cilantro and extra chili and serve with lime wedges.

Nutrition per serving:
842 cals / 46.25g fat / 99.17g carbs / 12.77g protein

BANANA PANCAKES

QUICK WHITE BEAN SALAD

COCONUT NOODLE SOUP WITH CHILI & LIME

WEEK THREE
WEEKLY SHOPPING LIST

FRUIT & VEG
- [ ] green apple – 1
- [ ] nectarine – 1
- [ ] watermelon – small wedge
- [ ] mango – 1
- [ ] plum – 1
- [ ] passionfruit – 1
- [ ] strawberries – 7
- [ ] bananas – 1
- [ ] cherry tomatoes – 8
- [ ] avocados – 2
- [ ] cucumber – ½
- [ ] yellow bell pepper – ½
- [ ] baby beets – 2
- [ ] eggplants – 2
- [ ] baby carrots – 1 bunch
- [ ] potato – 1
- [ ] red onion – 1
- [ ] zucchini – 1
- [ ] onions – 2 small
- [ ] celery – 1 stalk
- [ ] carrots – 2
- [ ] kale (if none left over from last week)
- [ ] beansprouts
- [ ] mushrooms – 3–4 large
- [ ] baby spinach leaves – 2 oz
- [ ] parsnip – 1
- [ ] lettuce
- [ ] tomato – 1
- [ ] sweet potatoes – 2 small
- [ ] garlic – 7 cloves
- [ ] ginger – 1½ inch piece
- [ ] fennel bulb – 1 (large – use for both recipes; or 2 small)
- [ ] scallions – 5
- [ ] Chinese cabbage (wombok)
- [ ] lemons – 3
- [ ] lime – 1
- [ ] green beans – 3½ oz
- [ ] broccolini – 1 bunch
- [ ] thyme – 1 bunch
- [ ] oregano
- [ ] rosemary
- [ ] flat-leaf parsley – 3 tablespoons
- [ ] basil – 1 bunch
- [ ] pomegranate – 1
- [ ] winter squash – ½
- [ ] asparagus – 6 spears
- [ ] dill – 2 teaspoons
- [ ] mint – 4–5 leaves
- [ ] cilantro – 1 stem

CHILLED/FROZEN
- [ ] coconut/plant-based yogurt – 7½ oz
- [ ] soy milk
- [ ] frozen mixed berries – 8¼ oz
- [ ] almond milk (or make, p.8) – 15 fl oz
- [ ] frozen green peas
- [ ] extra firm tofu – 5½ oz
- [ ] frozen spinach

CHECK TO SEE IF IN PANTRY
- [ ] coconut milk – 3½ fl oz tinned
- [ ] rolled (porridge) oats
- [ ] Puy lentils – 2¼ oz
- [ ] green lentils – 3 oz
- [ ] dried chickpeas
- [ ] quinoa flakes
- [ ] sushi rice
- [ ] brown rice
- [ ] wild rice
- [ ] quinoa
- [ ] sweetcorn kernels – 4½ oz
- [ ] toasted hazelnuts – 1 oz
- [ ] flaked almonds
- [ ] nori sheets – 2
- [ ] kombu (dried kelp) – 1 piece
- [ ] nori furikake
- [ ] sesame seeds
- [ ] chia seeds
- [ ] ground hemp seeds
- [ ] garam masala
- [ ] chili flakes
- [ ] black sesame seeds
- [ ] bay leaf
- [ ] ground turmeric
- [ ] ground cumin
- [ ] ground coriander
- [ ] ground cardamom
- [ ] cinnamon stick
- [ ] finely shredded coconut
- [ ] coconut flakes
- [ ] white miso paste
- [ ] coconut cream
- [ ] coconut sugar
- [ ] raw (demerara) sugar
- [ ] natural vanilla extract
- [ ] maple syrup
- [ ] self-rising flour
- [ ] sesame flour
- [ ] chickpea flour (besan)
- [ ] all-purpose flour
- [ ] olive oil
- [ ] vegetable oil
- [ ] toasted sesame oil
- [ ] coconut oil
- [ ] rice vinegar
- [ ] mirin
- [ ] tahini
- [ ] tamari
- [ ] sake
- [ ] nutritional yeast flakes
- [ ] acai powder
- [ ] vanilla protein powder
- [ ] panko breadcrumbs
- [ ] sourdough bread – 2 slices (or frozen left-over slices)
- [ ] burger bun – 1
- [ ] kimchi
- [ ] Sriracha sauce

WEEK 3 PREP

Check to see if you have any of these items already made and if not, add ingredients to your shopping list.

BASICS
(these are items that you should have pre-prepped as they will last a while)
- [ ] Banana bread loaf (p.34)
- [ ] Roasted sumac chickpeas (p.24)
- [ ] Granola (p.32)
- [ ] Vegan broth (p.30)
- [ ] Almond milk (p.8)
- [ ] Crunchy seed mix (p.24)
- [ ] Eggplant caponata (p.22)
- [ ] Piccalilli (p.20)
- [ ] Chargrilled eggplant & sumac dip (p.40)

PREP
- [ ] Soak chickpeas (DAY 17)

MAKE
- [ ] Vegan aïoli DAY 15 (p.18)
- [ ] Chargrilled eggplant & sumac dip DAY 21 (p.40)
- [ ] Chermoula DAY 15 (p.28)
- [ ] Chickpea flour crêpes DAY 20 (p.36)
- [ ] Pico de gallo DAY 21 (p.28)

COOK
- [ ] Quinoa (DAY 21)

WEEK 3 TIMETABLE

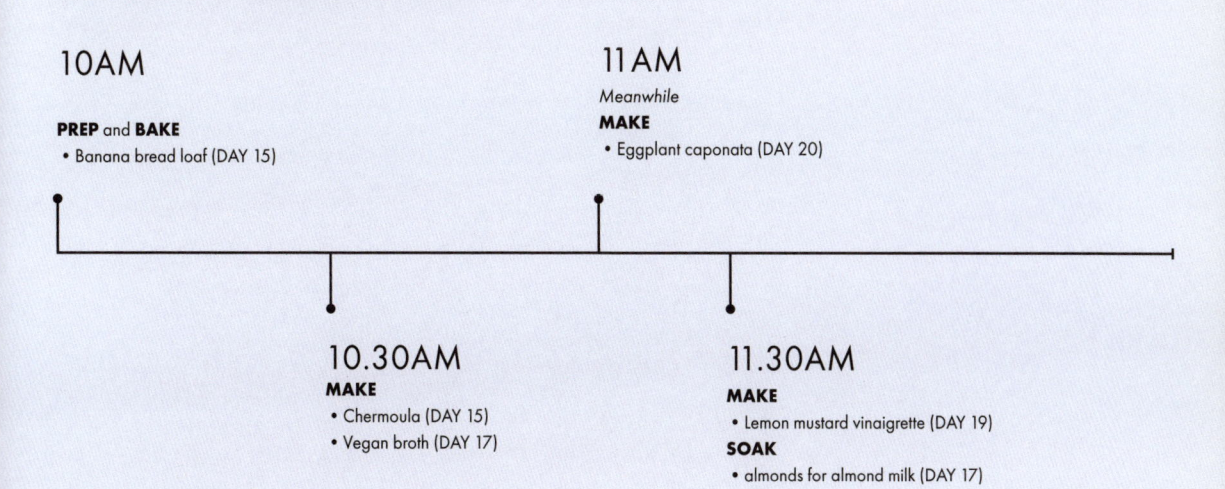

10AM
PREP and **BAKE**
- Banana bread loaf (DAY 15)

10.30AM
MAKE
- Chermoula (DAY 15)
- Vegan broth (DAY 17)

11AM
Meanwhile
MAKE
- Eggplant caponata (DAY 20)

11.30AM
MAKE
- Lemon mustard vinaigrette (DAY 19)

SOAK
- almonds for almond milk (DAY 17)

DAY 15

WEEK 3
MONDAY

Freeze extra slices of the banana bread individually for snacks on other days or quick breakfasts. Set the left-over sushi rolls aside for another time.

BREAKFAST
Toasted banana bread

SERVES: 1
PREP / COOK TIME
5 minutes / 5 minutes

2 slices of Banana bread loaf (p.34)
1 tablespoon coconut yogurt
1 tablespoon toasted coconut flakes
1 teaspoon maple syrup

01 Toast banana bread. Serve with yogurt, coconut flakes and a drizzle of maple syrup.

Nutrition per serving:
531 cals / 20.29g fat / 81.63g carbs / 11.05g protein

LUNCH
Sushi hand rolls

MAKES: 4 HAND ROLLS
PREP / COOK TIME
10 minutes / 25 minutes

2¾ oz sushi rice, rinsed
1 piece of kombu (dried kelp)
1 tablespoon rice vinegar
2 sheets of nori, cut in half
½ avocado
½ cucumber, cut thinly lengthways
½ yellow bell pepper
1 teaspoon nori furikake
1 tablespoon Vegan aïoli (p.18)

01 Place rice in a small pan, cover with 3 fl oz water and add kombu. Cover and bring to the boil. Reduce heat and simmer for 10–12 minutes until water is absorbed. Remove from heat and keep covered for 10 minutes. Uncover, remove kombu and add vinegar. Stir to fluff up rice.

02 Lay nori sheets on a work surface, shiny side down. Scoop 3 tablespoons of rice onto first edge of nori and flatten into a triangle shape over nori. Layer with fillings and wrap lower corner of nori up and over, then roll to create a cone. Dampen finger and run along last edge of nori or use a few grains of rice to seal. Serve.

Nutrition per serving:
525 cals / 17.52g fat / 83.96g carbs / 10.39g protein

DINNER
Warm roasted root vegetables with chermoula

SERVES: 1
PREP / COOK TIME
10 minutes / 30 minutes

2 baby beets, quartered
1 bunch of baby carrots, trimmed
1 parsnip, quartered
1 small sweet potato, cut into wedges
2 garlic cloves
½ tablespoon olive oil
1 teaspoon salt
2 tablespoons Chermoula (p.28)
2 tablespoons Roasted sumac chickpeas (p.24)

01 Preheat oven to 375°F. Place cut vegetables and garlic on a lined baking tray. Drizzle with oil and sprinkle with salt. Toss to coat evenly and roast for 25–30 minutes, turning halfway through until softened and caramelizing on the edges.

02 Transfer vegetables to a serving bowl and top with chermoula and chickpeas.

Nutrition per serving:
362 cals / 16.59g fat / 51.02g carbs / 5.94g protein

TOASTED BANANA BREAD

SUSHI HAND ROLLS

WARM ROASTED ROOT VEGETABLES WITH CHERMOULA

DAY 16

WEEK 3
TUESDAY

The creamy vegetable bake for tonight's dinner is a delicious, comforting meal. Warm and full of mixed vegetables, it will become a regular on your menu. Save extras for a side dish over the next day or two.

Granola cup

SERVES: 1
PREP / COOK TIME
5 minutes / 0 minutes

1 tablespoon vanilla protein powder
¼ cup coconut or other plant-based yogurt
2 oz Granola (p.32)
1 nectarine, stoned and sliced
3 strawberries, sliced

01 Mix protein powder with yogurt and layer with granola and fruits in a glass or bowl. Serve immediately so granola doesn't lose its crunch from the moisture in yogurt.

Nutrition per serving:
398 cals / 16.77g fat / 64.88g carbs / 19.86g protein

Fennel & apple Asian slaw with sesame

SERVES: 1
PREP / COOK TIME
10 minutes / 0 minutes

1¾ oz extra firm tofu (optional)
½ green apple
1 oz Chinese cabbage (wombok)
½ small fennel bulb, plus fronds
1 small scallion, sliced
1 tablespoon lemon juice
½ teaspoon toasted sesame oil
1 tablespoon mirin
1 tablespoon rice vinegar
1 tablespoon black sesame seeds
2 tablespoons flaked almonds

01 Grate tofu, if using, and set aside. Use a food processor or mandoline to finely shave/chop apple, cabbage and fennel. Place in a large bowl and toss together with scallion and lemon juice.

02 In a separate small bowl, combine sesame oil, mirin and vinegar. Pour over slaw and mix to combine, then sprinkle with sesame seeds, flaked almonds and grated tofu, if liked.

Nutrition per serving:
400 cals / 23.68g fat / 33.27g carbs / 16.69g protein

Vegetable bake

SERVES: 2
PREP / COOK TIME
10 minutes / 40 minutes

1 potato
1 small sweet potato
¾ oz baby spinach leaves
1 small eggplant, thinly sliced
3–4 large mushrooms, sliced
coconut oil, for oiling
5 fl oz soy milk
1 tablespoon chickpea flour (besan)
1 thyme sprig, leaves picked
1 garlic clove, crushed
1 tablespoon nutritional yeast flakes
salt and pepper

01 Preheat oven to 400°F. Peel and thinly slice potatoes, then layer with spinach, eggplant and mushrooms into an oiled baking dish, seasoning as you go.

02 Whisk milk, flour, thyme, garlic and yeast flakes together in a pan. Stir over medium heat until sauce thickens. Pour over vegetables and season. Cover with foil and bake for 25 minutes. Uncover and cook for 10–15 minutes until crisp on top.

Nutrition per serving:
318 cals / 4.32g fat / 62.67g carbs / 12.04g protein

GRANOLA CUP

FENNEL & APPLE ASIAN SLAW WITH SESAME

VEGETABLE BAKE

DAY 17

WEEK 3
WEDNESDAY

You can add extra greens to the lunch if you have them or prefer a specific type. Add any leftovers from the lunch to the curry, if you like.

Mixed berry on-the-go smoothie

SERVES: 1
PREP / COOK TIME
5 minutes / 0 minutes

3½–5½ oz frozen mixed berries
2 tablespoons acai powder
2 tablespoons rolled (porridge) oats
9–10 fl oz almond milk (p.8)
1 handful of baby spinach leaves

01 Blend together frozen berries, acai powder, oats, milk and spinach leaves. Add more milk to achieve your preferred thickness.

Nutrition per serving:
629 cals / 26.38g fat / 72.83g carbs / 14.97g protein

Charred beans & broccolini tahini salad

SERVES: 1
PREP / COOK TIME
10 minutes / 10 minutes

3½ oz green beans
½ bunch of broccolini
1 tablespoon toasted sesame oil
¼ oz toasted hazelnuts, chopped

Lemon tahini dressing:
2 tablespoons tahini
1 tablespoon lemon juice
1 teaspoon grated lemon zest

01 Whisk dressing ingredients together with 1 tablespoon water in a bowl until smooth.

02 Blanch beans and broccolini in boiling water for 2 minutes, then refresh in iced water. Heat a pan over high heat, add oil and beans and broccolini and fry so they cook slightly and char on the edges. Serve with dressing drizzled over top and sprinkled with hazelnuts.

Nutrition per serving:
388 cals / 36.32g fat / 13.54g carbs / 7.92g protein

Squash curry

SERVES: 1
PREP / COOK TIME
10 minutes / 30 minutes

½ teaspoon ground turmeric
½ teaspoon ground cumin
½ teaspoon ground coriander
¼ teaspoon ground cardamon
1 cinnamon stick
pinch of chili flakes (optional)
½ tablespoon coconut oil
½ red onion, sliced
1¾ oz dried chickpeas, soaked overnight
5 fl oz coconut cream
7 fl oz Vegan broth (p.30) or water
1¾ oz winter squash, peeled and cubed
1 tablespoon toasted coconut flakes
1 tablespoon Crunchy seed mix (p.24)
salt

01 Combine spices in bowl. Heat oil in a pan and fry onion briefly before adding spices. Stir, then add chickpeas, coconut cream and broth. Cover and bring to the boil. Reduce heat and simmer for 10 minutes. Stir, add squash and cook until soft. Season, then serve with coconut flakes and seed mix.

Nutrition per serving:
757 cals / 57.32g fat / 54.16g carbs / 18.33g protein

MIXED BERRY ON-THE-GO SMOOTHIE

CHARRED BEANS & BROCCOLINI TAHINI SALAD

SQUASH CURRY

DAY 18

WEEK 3
THURSDAY

Quinoa flakes are so fine, they cook quickly. Have the banana ready and you will be eating a warm, tasty breakfast in minutes.

Quinoa banana porridge

SERVES: 1
PREP / COOK TIME
5 minutes / 5 minutes

1½ oz quinoa flakes
½ cup almond milk or other plant-based milk (p.8)
1 banana, mashed
1 tablespoon ground hemp seeds

01 Add quinoa flakes to a small pan with milk and 3½ fl oz water. Heat over low heat for 5 minutes, stirring occasionally as flakes cook and mixture thickens. Add more liquid if you prefer it less thick. Stir through mashed banana, then sprinkle with ground hemp seeds to serve.

Nutrition per serving:
343 cals / 7.47g fat / 63.32g carbs / 9.14g protein

Tofu & spinach saag

SERVES: 1
PREP / COOK TIME
5 minutes / 15 minutes

½ tablespoon coconut oil
2¾ oz firm tofu, pressed and cubed
½ small onion, diced
2 garlic cloves, finely diced
½ teaspoon garam masala
¼ teaspoon ground cumin
¼ teaspoon ground turmeric
3½ fl oz coconut milk
2¾ oz frozen spinach
sea salt and pepper

01 Heat oil in a pan and pan-fry tofu cubes until golden on all sides. Remove from pan, add onion and garlic and fry for 2 minutes until translucent. Add spices, stir to combine, then add coconut milk, spinach and tofu. Season and simmer for 10 minutes before serving.

Nutrition per serving:
413 cals / 35.32g fat / 15.32g carbs / 16.84g protein

Lentil pilaf with flaked almonds & herbs

SERVES: 2
PREP / COOK TIME
5 minutes / 40 minutes

1 tablespoon olive oil
3 scallions, chopped
1 garlic clove, finely chopped
2¼ oz Puy lentils, rinsed
1¾ oz brown rice, rinsed
1 oz wild rice, rinsed
2 thyme sprigs, leaves picked
1½ cups Vegan broth (p.30)
2 tablespoons flaked almonds
2 tablespoons chopped flat-leaf parsley
2 tablespoons pomegranate seeds

01 Heat oil in a large pan and fry scallions, garlic, lentils and rices for 4–5 minutes. Add thyme and broth and bring to the boil. Reduce heat, cover and simmer for 30 minutes, or until liquid is absorbed and rice and lentils tender. Add flaked almonds and parsley in last 5 minutes of cooking. Sprinkle with pomegranate seeds. Store leftovers in fridge for another time.

Nutrition per serving:
296.5 cals / 9.19g fat / 49.88g carbs / 07.52g protein

QUINOA BANANA PORRIDGE

LENTIL PILAF WITH FLAKED ALMONDS & HERBS

TOFU & SPINACH SAAG

DAY 19

WEEK 3
FRIDAY

Eggplants have a great texture and flavor and when baked in this recipe they become caramelized and delicious. They can also be cooked on the barbecue.

Summer fruit salad

SERVES: 1
PREP / COOK TIME
5 minutes / 0 minutes

- 1 slice watermelon, diced
- 1 mango, cheeks diced
- 4 strawberries, halved
- 1 plum, stoned and sliced
- 4–5 mint leaves
- 1 passionfruit

01 Combine sliced fruits in a bowl with mint leaves. Spoon over passionfruit pulp to serve.

Nutrition per serving:
314 cals / 23.24g fat / 28.52g carbs / 4g protein

Quinoa, asparagus & roasted tomato salad

SERVES: 1
PREP / COOK TIME
10 minutes / 45 minutes

- 8 cherry tomatoes, halved
- ½ tablespoon olive oil
- 6 asparagus spears, halved
- 2 oz quinoa
- 6–7 basil leaves, chopped
- 1 tablespoon Lemon mustard vinaigrette (p.16)
- 2 tablespoons Roasted sumac chickpeas (p.24)
- sea salt and pepper

01 Preheat oven to 320°F. Place tomatoes on a baking tray and drizzle with oil. Season. Roast for 25 minutes, add asparagus and toss to coat in oil. Cook until tomatoes are caramelized.

02 Meanwhile, add quinoa to a pan, cover with 11 fl oz water and bring to the boil. Reduce heat, cover and cook for 10 minutes. Stir to fluff up. Add basil and vinaigrette and stir. Mix in tomatoes and asparagus, then top with chickpeas and serve.

Nutrition per serving:
329 cals / 11.39g fat / 46.34g carbs / 12.54g protein

Miso-glazed eggplant

SERVES: 1
PREP / COOK TIME
15 minutes / 25 minutes

- 1 medium eggplant, halved lengthways
- 1 teaspoon salt
- ½ tablespoon toasted sesame seeds
- 1 cilantro stem, leaves picked
- 1 scallion, sliced

Glaze:
- 1 tablespoon mirin
- 1 tablespoon sake
- ½ tablespoon raw (demerara) sugar or maple syrup
- 1 teaspoon toasted sesame oil
- 1 heaped tablespoon white miso paste
- 1 teaspoon finely grated ginger

01 Preheat oven to 375°F. Score eggplant halves in criss-cross pattern. Rub salt over flesh and leave for 10 minutes in a baking dish. Whisk glaze ingredients together, then brush generously over eggplant. Bake for 25 minutes. Brush more glaze over top, then sprinkle with sesame seeds, cilantro and scallion.

Nutrition per serving:
275 cals / 8.49g fat / 44.08g carbs / 8.45g protein

SUMMER FRUIT SALAD

MISO-GLAZED EGGPLANT

QUINOA, ASPARAGUS & ROASTED TOMATO SALAD

DAY 20

WEEK 3
SATURDAY

There's nothing better than a lazy Saturday morning breakfast of pancakes. Save the leftovers in the fridge for a snack later over the weekend or store the batter in the fridge for up to 5 days.

Crêpes with mixed berry coulis

SERVES: 2
PREP / COOK TIME
10 minutes / 15 minutes

2¾ oz frozen mixed berries
½ tablespoon coconut sugar
1 tablespoon lemon juice
1 quantity Chickpea flour crêpe (p.36)
2 tablespoons all-purpose flour
2 tablespoons maple syrup
coconut oil, for oiling

01 Bring berries, sugar, lemon juice and 2 tablespoons water slowly to a simmer in a pan, stirring occasionally and using back of a spoon to push down on berries as they cook.

02 Mix together crêpe ingredients with the flour and maple syrup. Heat a crêpe pan over medium heat and grease well with oil. Pour some of the batter onto pan and spread thinly. Cook for 2–3 minutes until edges start to pull away from pan. Flip and cook other side for 1–2 minutes. Remove and repeat with remaining mixture. Drizzle with berry coulis and serve.

Nutrition per serving:
354 cals / 7.14g fat / 59.43g carbs / 13.24g protein

Piccalilli snack plate

SERVES: 1
PREP / COOK TIME
10 minutes / 0 minutes

¼ small fennel bulb, shaved
1 teaspoon olive oil
2 teaspoons chopped dill
½ avocado, pitted and sliced
3 tablespoons Piccalilli (p.20)
2 slices crusty sourdough bread
salt and pepper

01 Mix fennel, oil and dill together in a bowl. Season and toss to coat.

02 Serve fennel mix, avocado and piccalilli on a plate with sourdough.

Nutrition per serving:
426 cals / 21.75g fat / 52.58g carbs / 11.48g protein

Lentil burgers

SERVES: 2
PREP / COOK TIME
10 minutes / 35 minutes

3 oz green lentils
1 small carrot, finely diced
1 small onion, finely diced
1 celery stalk, finely diced
1 garlic clove
1 bay leaf
½ teaspoon salt
½ teaspoon ground cumin
1 teaspoon oregano leaves
2¾ oz panko breadcrumbs
1 tablespoon olive oil
1 burger bun, 1 lettuce leaf, 2 slices tomato, ½ avocado, Eggplant caponata (p.22), Vegan aïoli (p.18), to serve

01 Bring lentils, vegetables, garlic, bay leaf, 1 cup water, salt, cumin and oregano to the boil in a pan. Reduce heat and simmer for 20 minutes. Stir in three-quarters of breadcrumbs, remove bay leaf and blend mix until smooth. Shape into 2 patties and coat in remaining breadcrumbs. Heat oil in a frying pan and brown patties on each side. Serve in burger bun with toppings of your choice. Keep second burger in the fridge for another time.

Nutrition per serving:
454 cals / 17.72g fat / 64.57g carbs / 14.2g protein

CRÊPES WITH MIXED BERRY COULIS

PICCALILLI SNACK PLATE

LENTIL BURGERS

DAY 21

WEEK 3
SUNDAY

Tonight's fried rice is a good recipe to add extra vegetables to if you have any that need using up. Store left-over breakfast in the fridge for later.

Zucchini & corn cakes with pico de gallo

SERVES: 2
PREP / COOK TIME
15 minutes / 15 minutes

4½ oz frozen sweetcorn kernels, thawed (or tinned)
1 zucchini, grated
½ red onion
2½ oz self-rising flour
2 tablespoons vegetable oil
salt and pepper
2 heaped tablespoons Pico de gallo (p.28)
lime wedges, to serve

01 Divide sweetcorn and blend half along with zucchini, onion and flour in a food processor until smooth. Transfer to a bowl. Season well and add remaining corn.

02 Heat a nonstick frying pan, add half the oil and swirl pan to coat. Scoop 3 tablespoons batter into pan and fry for 2 minutes. Reduce heat slightly and cook until edges start to firm. Flip over to cook other side. Remove and repeat with rest of batter. Serve with pico de gallo and lime.

Nutrition per serving:
304 cals / 14.81g fat / 39.25g carbs / 8.2g protein

Roasted squash with eggplant dip

SERVES: 1
PREP / COOK TIME
5 minutes / 25 minutes

1 tablespoon olive oil
3 winter squash wedges
1 rosemary sprig, leaves picked
1 oz baby spinach leaves
2 tablespoons Chargrilled eggplant & sumac dip (p.40)
1 tablespoon toasted hazelnuts, roughly chopped
1 tablespoon Crunchy seed mix (optional) (p.24)
1 tablespoon chopped flat-leaf parsley
salt

01 Preheat oven to 350°F. Brush oil over squash, season with salt and sprinkle with rosemary leaves. Place on a lined baking tray and bake for 20–25 minutes until softened.

02 Sit squash on a plate on top of spinach. Serve dip on top and sprinkle with nuts, seeds, if using, and parsley.

Nutrition per serving:
429 cals / 37.95g fat / 21.22g carbs / 10.15g protein

Kimchi fried quinoa

SERVES: 1
PREP / COOK TIME
10 minutes / 10 minutes

1 teaspoon toasted sesame oil
1 teaspoon finely grated ginger
1 oz kimchi, finely chopped
1 curly kale stalk, leaves thinly sliced
1½ oz frozen green peas
1½ oz cooked quinoa
1 small carrot, grated
3 tablespoons beansprouts
½ tablespoon tamari
½ tablespoon Sriracha sauce, or to taste

01 Heat oil in a frying pan over medium-high heat and fry ginger, kimchi, kale and peas for 2 minutes to release flavor. Add quinoa, carrot and sprouts. Pour sauces over and toss well to heat through and coat with sauce.

02 Serve hot with extra chili sauce as liked.

Nutrition per serving:
281 cals / 7.76g fat / 43.43g carbs / 11.24g protein

ZUCCHINI & CORN CAKES WITH PICO DE GALLO

ROASTED SQUASH WITH EGGPLANT DIP

KIMCHI FRIED QUINOA

WEEK FOUR
WEEKLY SHOPPING LIST

FRUIT & VEG
- beansprouts
- carrots – 4
- zucchini – 2
- celery – 3 stalks
- garlic – 1 bulb
- potatoes – 2
- thyme
- baby romaine lettuce – 1 head
- iceberg lettuce – 1
- sweetcorn – 1 cob
- scallions – 4
- French breakfast radishes – 2
- red chilies – 2
- oyster mushrooms – 4
- shiitake mushroom – 1
- enoki mushrooms – 1 bunch
- curly kale – 1 leaf & 1 stalk
- flat-leaf parsley – 1 bunch
- cilantro – 1 bunch
- basil
- lemons – 5
- limes – 3
- avocados – 3
- cauliflower – ½
- onion – 1 small
- red bell pepper – 1
- mango – 1
- strawberries (if none left over)
- roma (plum) tomatoes – 3
- Persian cucumber – 1
- jalapeño – 1
- French shallots – 6
- red cabbage – ¼
- green apple – 1
- bananas – 2
- spinach leaf – 1 large
- Chinese cabbage (wombok)
- baby spinach leaves – ½ oz
- nectarine – 1
- mint – 1 bunch
- eggplant – 1 small
- button mushrooms – 2–3
- passionfruit – 1

CHILLED/FROZEN
- soy milk – ½ cup
- coconut/soy yogurt – 1¾ fl oz
- extra firm tofu – 8 oz
- frozen acai purée – 3½ oz

CHECK TO SEE IF IN PANTRY
- silken tofu – 1½ oz
- rolled (porridge) oats
- diced tomatoes – 1 lb 7 oz tinned
- jackfruit – 14 oz tinned
- baked beans – 8 oz tinned
- sweetcorn kernels – 1½ oz tinned
- black beans – 3½ oz tinned
- green lentils – 3½ oz
- chickpeas – 2lb 10 oz tinned
- quinoa – 1½ oz
- pearl barley – 1¾ oz
- sticky glutinous rice – 2½ oz
- wild rice – 3½ oz
- fried tofu puffs
- vermicelli noodles – 1¾ oz
- peanut butter (or make, p.8)
- almond butter (or make, p.8)
- almonds
- pine nuts
- pecans
- walnuts – 1¾ oz
- flaked almonds
- ground flaxseeds
- chia seeds
- ground hemp seeds
- coconut flakes
- dried apricots
- prunes
- green olives – 8
- coconut milk – tinned (9½ fl oz)
- cloves
- ground cinnamon
- nutmeg
- chili flakes
- smoked paprika
- dried mixed herbs
- natural vanilla extract
- ground cumin
- ground turmeric
- raw (demerara) sugar
- maple syrup
- sesame seeds
- white miso paste
- hoisin sauce
- light soy sauce
- barbecue sauce
- passata (tomato purée)
- coconut oil
- olive oil
- nut or sunflower oil
- toasted sesame oil
- coconut oil
- avocado oil
- red wine vinegar
- rice vinegar
- mirin
- vegan laksa paste
- pickled jalapeños
- self-rising flour
- cream of tartar
- baking soda
- vanilla protein powder
- soft tacos – 4–6
- large tortilla wrap – 1
- sourdough bread – 1 loaf
- panko breadcrumbs
- nutritional yeast flakes

WEEK 4 PREP

Check to see if you have any of these items already made and if not, add ingredients to your shopping list.

BASICS
(these are items that you should have pre-prepped as they will last a while)
- [ ] Carrot & parsnip loaf (p.34)
- [ ] Peanut butter (p.8)
- [ ] Almond butter (p.8)
- [ ] Roasted sumac chickpeas (p.24)
- [ ] Eggplant caponata (p.22)
- [ ] Beet hummus (p.40)
- [ ] Sauerkraut (p.20)
- [ ] Vegan broth (p.30)
- [ ] Crunchy seed mix (p.24) if none left over

PREP
- [ ] Soak prunes (DAY 25)
- [ ] Soak sticky rice (DAY 23)

MAKE
- [ ] Lemon mustard vinaigrette DAY 22 (p.16)
- [ ] Tofu miso dressing DAY 23 (p.18)
- [ ] Sesame rice wine dressing DAY 24 (p.16)
- [ ] Guacamole DAY 26 (p.40)
- [ ] Vegan meatloaf DAY 22 (p.106)
- [ ] Coconut yogurt lime chili dressing DAY 28 (p.18)
- [ ] Lentil vegetable soup DAY 23 (p.108)

COOK
- [ ] Wild rice (DAYS 24 & 25)

WEEK 4 TIMETABLE

10AM
PREP and **BAKE**
- Vegan meatloaf (DAY 22)

10.30AM
MAKE
- Tofu miso dressing (DAY 23)
- Sesame rice wine dressing (DAY 24)
- Coconut yogurt lime chili dressing (DAY 28)

10.45AM
Meanwhile
MAKE
- Lentil vegetable soup (DAY 23)

11.15AM
COOK
- wild rice (DAYS 24 & 25)

SOAK
- prunes (DAY 25)

DAY 22

WEEK 4
MONDAY

If you haven't tried it yet, make your own nut butter to go with the breakfast loaf today. Freeze the left-over meatloaf for another time.

Carrot & parsnip loaf with peanut butter

SERVES: 1
PREP / COOK TIME
5 minutes / 5 minutes

- 2 slices Carrot & parsnip loaf (p.34)
- 2–3 tablespoons peanut (or other nut) butter (p.8)
- 3 strawberries, sliced

01 Carefully toast loaf slices. Spread slices with peanut butter and sliced strawberries.

Nutrition per serving:
664 cals / 28.84g fat / 67.48g carbs / 16.69g protein

Lemon romaine salad

SERVES: 1
PREP / COOK TIME
10 minutes / 0 minutes

- 1 head baby romaine lettuce, roughly chopped
- 1 sweetcorn cob, kernels removed
- 1 scallion, sliced
- 2 French breakfast radishes, finely shaved
- 2 flat-leaf parsley sprigs, leaves picked and roughly chopped
- 3 tablespoons Lemon mustard vinaigrette (p.16)

01 Combine all ingredients in a bowl and toss so lettuce is coated well in dressing. Serve.

Nutrition per serving:
298 cals / 6.13g fat / 65g carbs / 11.7g protein

Vegan meatloaf

SERVES: 2
PREP / COOK TIME
10 minutes / 45 minutes

- ½ tablespoon avocado oil
- ½ small onion
- 1 small carrot, grated
- 1 small zucchini, grated
- 1 celery stalk, diced
- 2 garlic cloves, crushed
- 14 oz tinned chickpeas, drained
- 1¾ oz panko breadcrumbs
- 1½ tablespoons ground flaxseeds
- 2 tablespoons nutritional yeast flakes
- 2 tablespoons barbecue sauce
- 2 tablespoons passata (tomato purée)
- 1 teaspoon ground cumin
- ½ teaspoon ground turmeric
- Eggplant caponata (p.22) and ¼ oz chopped flat-leaf parsley, to serve

01 Preheat oven to 350°F. Heat oil in a pan and fry vegetables and garlic for 5–6 minutes. Mash chickpeas a little, then mix with vegetables and remaining ingredients. Transfer to a lined 7½ x 3½ inch loaf tin. Cover with foil. Bake for 20 minutes. Uncover and bake until golden. Leave for 10 minutes. Serve with caponata and parsley.

Nutrition per serving:
443 cals / 10.9g fat / 71.37g carbs / 22.38g protein

CARROT & PARSNIP LOAF WITH PEANUT BUTTER

LEMON ROMAINE SALAD

VEGAN MEATLOAF

DAY 23

WEEK 4
TUESDAY

The soup for dinner is so adaptable — add more or different vegetables or change the herbs and spices. Freeze leftovers for later.

Coconut sticky rice pudding

SERVES: 1
PREP / COOK TIME
5 minutes + overnight soaking / 15 minutes

2½ oz white sticky rice
⅓ cup coconut milk
1 tablespoon maple syrup
1 mango cheek (or other seasonal fruit), cut into bite-sized chunks
1 passionfruit

01 Cover rice in water and soak overnight.

02 The next day, drain and rinse rice and add to a small pan with 2¼ fl oz water and three-quarters of the coconut milk. Bring mixture to the boil, reduce heat, cover and cook for 10 minutes. Check to make sure liquid has been absorbed, if not cook for another few minutes. Turn off heat but leave lid on for another 5 minutes to steam.

03 Stir remaining coconut milk and maple syrup through hot rice and serve with mango chunks and passionfruit pulp.

Nutrition per serving:
544 cals / 10.9g fat / 88.3g carbs / 18.85g protein

Tofu miso red cabbage slaw

SERVES: 1
PREP / COOK TIME
10 minutes / 0 minutes

7 oz red cabbage, finely shaved
½ green apple, cut into fine matchsticks
1 carrot, cut into fine matchsticks
1 tablespoon toasted sesame seeds
2–3 tablespoons Tofu miso dressing (p.18)

01 Combine all ingredients in a bowl and toss together. Add more dressing as needed.

Nutrition per serving:
246 cals / 6.95g fat / 43.68g carbs / 8.08g protein

Lentil vegetable soup

SERVES: 2
PREP / COOK TIME
10 minutes / 35 minutes

1 tablespoon olive oil
½ small onion, diced
1 garlic clove, crushed
1 small carrot, sliced
1 celery stalk, sliced
2 potatoes, roughly chopped
2 thyme sprigs, leaves picked
12 fl oz Vegan broth (p.30)
3½ oz green lentils
9 oz tinned diced tomatoes
1 teaspoon sea salt
pepper
2 flat-leaf parsley sprigs, leaves chopped, to serve

01 Heat oil in a pan and fry onion, garlic, carrot and celery for 4–5 minutes, stirring occasionally so garlic doesn't burn. Add potatoes and thyme and season well. Cook for 2 minutes before adding broth. Bring to the boil, then reduce heat to continue simmering. Add lentils and diced tomatoes, cover and cook for 20–25 minutes until lentils and vegetables have softened. Season to taste and serve with parsley.

Nutrition per serving:
433 cals / 7.6g fat / 83.53g carbs / 13.39g protein

COCONUT STICKY RICE PUDDING

TOFU MISO RED CABBAGE SLAW

LENTIL VEGETABLE SOUP

DAY 24

WEEK 4
WEDNESDAY

While you are cooking rice for the dinner tonight, save time and make extra to use for tomorrow's lunch.

Almond butter & banana toast

SERVES: 1
PREP / COOK TIME
5 minutes / 5 minutes

2 slices sourdough or preferred bread
2–3 tablespoons almond butter (p.8)
1 banana, sliced
2 teaspoons ground hemp seeds

01 Toast bread and spread with almond butter. Top with banana slices and sprinkle with ground hemp seeds.

Nutrition per serving:
1133 cals / 31.43g fat / 80.15g carbs / 33.39g protein

Minced tofu lettuce cups

SERVES: 1
PREP / COOK TIME
10 minutes / 10 minutes

1 oz extra firm tofu
½ teaspoon toasted sesame oil
1 small carrot, finely diced
1 celery stalk, finely diced
2 oyster mushrooms, finely diced
1 scallion, thinly sliced
1 red chili, thinly sliced
1 teaspoon light soy sauce
2 teaspoons hoisin sauce
¼ oz cilantro leaves, roughly chopped
2 iceberg lettuce leaves, cut to bowl size
lime wedges, to serve

01 Press tofu with paper towel to drain any excess water and use your fingertips to crumble. Heat oil in a frying pan over medium–high heat and fry carrot, celery and mushrooms for 4–5 minutes. Add tofu, half the scallion, chili, soy and hoisin and stir-fry to heat through. Remove from heat, add cilantro and serve in lettuce cups, topped with remaining scallion and lime wedges.

Nutrition per serving:
300 cals / 15.09g fat / 23.98g carbs / 23.64g protein

Wild rice with mixed mushrooms & kale

SERVES: 1
PREP / COOK TIME
10 minutes / 45 minutes

3½ oz wild rice
2 cups water or Vegan broth (p.30)
½ teaspoon salt
½ tablespoon coconut oil
1 garlic clove, thinly sliced
1 shiitake mushroom, sliced
2 oyster mushrooms, sliced
½ bunch of enoki mushrooms, trimmed
2–3 button mushrooms, halved
1 curly kale leaf, roughly chopped
2 tablespoons Sesame rice wine dressing (p.16)
2 flat-leaf parsley sprigs, leaves roughly chopped

01 Bring rice, water or broth and half the salt to the boil, then reduce heat, cover and cook for 40–45 minutes until rice has softened. Drain. Meanwhile heat oil in a pan and fry garlic for 1–2 minutes. Add mushrooms and cook for 6–8 minutes. Mix in kale and half the dressing. Reserve 3½ oz cooked rice for tomorrow and mix rest through mushrooms. Add rest of dressing and parsley.

Nutrition per serving:
358 cals / 8.89g fat / 53.91g carbs / 17.37g protein

**ALMOND BUTTER
& BANANA TOAST**

**MINCED TOFU
LETTUCE CUPS**

**WILD RICE WITH MIXED
MUSHROOMS & KALE**

DAY 25

WEEK 4
THURSDAY

Use the prune juice in today's breakfast for flavoring; keep it in a container in the fridge and add it to baking for a sweet flavor.

Granola with pecans & prunes

SERVES: 1
PREP / COOK TIME
10 minutes / 0 minutes

1¾ oz rolled (porridge) oats
1 oz pecans, roughly chopped
3 dried apricots, thinly sliced
3–4 prunes, soaked (see p.53)
3 tablespoons prune juice (from soaking)
1 tablespoon coconut or soy yogurt

01 Combine oats, pecans and apricots in a serving bowl. Top with prune juice and leave to stand for 5–10 minutes. Top with yogurt and prunes when ready to eat.

Nutrition per serving:
434 cals / 25.58g fat / 63.2g carbs / 12.85g protein

Rice salad with olives & almonds

SERVES: 1
PREP / COOK TIME
5 minutes / 10 minutes

2 tablespoons almonds
1 teaspoon coconut oil
½ teaspoon ground turmeric
1 scallion, sliced
1 spinach leaf, thinly chopped
1 tablespoon lemon juice
3½ oz left-over cooked wild rice (see p.110)
6–8 green olives, pitted and halved
1 teaspoon grated lemon zest
salt

01 Preheat oven to 350°F. Spread almonds out on a baking tray and toast for 6 minutes, or until golden and crunchy. Heat oil in a frying pan and fry turmeric and scallion for 1–2 minutes. Add spinach, lemon juice and salt and cook for a few minutes as spinach softens.

02 Combine rice and green olives in a bowl. Add spinach mix and top with lemon zest and roughly chopped almonds.

Nutrition per serving:
296 cals / 18.64g fat / 28.64g carbs / 8.89g protein

Tofu laksa

SERVES: 1
PREP / COOK TIME
5 minutes / 15 minutes

½ tablespoon coconut oil
2½ tablespoons vegan laksa paste
1 cup Vegan broth (p.30)
7 fl oz coconut milk
1¾ oz fried tofu puffs, halved
½ lime – 1 wedge for topping and remaining juiced
1¾ oz vermicelli noodles
¼ oz beansprouts
1 red chili, thinly sliced
1 handful of cilantro leaves

01 Heat oil in a pan and cook laksa paste for 1–2 minutes until fragrant. Add broth and coconut milk and simmer for 10 minutes. Add tofu puffs and lime juice in last couple of minutes so they soak up laksa flavor.

02 Cook noodles according to packet instructions. Rinse, drain and place noodles in serving bowl. Ladle laksa and tofu puffs over noodles and top with beansprouts, chili and cilantro.

Nutrition per serving:
709 cals / 40.07g fat / 65.24g carbs / 13.72g protein

RICE SALAD WITH OLIVES & ALMONDS

TOFU LAKSA

GRANOLA WITH PECANS & PRUNES

DAY 26

WEEK 4
FRIDAY

The gazpacho can easily be made ahead of time. Dinner makes extra pulled jackfruit to use for lunch tomorrow. It will keep for up to 4 days in the fridge.

Acai bowl with chia & toasted coconut

SERVES: 1
PREP / COOK TIME
5 minutes / 5 minutes

2 tablespoons coconut flakes
3½ oz frozen acai purée
1 frozen banana
½ cup soy milk
4–6 strawberries
1 tablespoon vanilla protein powder
1 tablespoon chia seeds

01 Preheat oven to 350°F. Spread coconut flakes out on a baking tray and bake for 4–5 minutes until toasted.

02 Meanwhile, blend acai, banana, milk, strawberries and protein powder until smooth in a blender. You may need to add a little extra milk, depending on how thick you like it to be. Pour into a bowl and top with toasted coconut and chia seeds.

Nutrition per serving:
498 cals / 17.61g fat / 75.58g carbs / 15.31g protein

Gazpacho

SERVES: 1
PREP / MARINATE TIME
10 minutes / 2–4 hours (optional)

1 slice crusty white sourdough bread, crust removed
2 large roma (plum) tomatoes, cored and halved
½ small Persian cucumber, peeled and halved
½ fresh jalapeño, seeded
1 French shallot
1 small garlic clove
1 tablespoon olive oil, plus extra for drizzling
2 teaspoons red wine vinegar
salt and pepper
1 tablespoon toasted pine nuts, for topping

01 Soak bread by running it under cold water for a second, then squeeze out all liquid. Add bread and remaining ingredients, except pine nuts, to a blender and blend until smooth. Taste and add extra seasoning as required. Either serve immediately or chill in a sealed container for a few hours to let the flavors develop.

02 Top with toasted pine nuts, black pepper and a drizzle of oil.

Nutrition per serving:
645 cals / 23.51g fat / 92.23g carbs / 20.27g protein

Pulled jackfruit tacos

SERVES: 2
PREP / COOK TIME
15 minutes / 45 minutes

2 French shallots, finely diced
½ teaspoon ground cumin
1 teaspoon smoked paprika
⅓ cup barbecue sauce
1 tablespoon passata (tomato purée)
14 oz tinned young jackfruit, drained
1¾ oz Chinese cabbage (wombok), finely shredded
2 tablespoons pickled jalapeños, sliced
¼ oz cilantro leaves, roughly chopped
1 tablespoon olive oil
4–6 soft tacos
4–6 tablespoons Guacamole (p.40)
sea salt and pepper
lime wedges, to serve

01 Cook shallots in ½ tablespoon water for a few minutes. Add spices, barbecue sauce, passata, jackfruit and 1 cup water. Bring to the boil, then cover and simmer until jackfruit is soft. Uncover and cook for 10–15 minutes to reduce liquid. Toss cabbage, jalapeños, cilantro, oil and seasoning together in a bowl. Layer each taco with jackfruit, guacamole and cabbage mix. Serve with lime. Store leftovers in fridge.

Nutrition per serving:
555 cals / 22.57g fat / 88.77g carbs / 8.24g protein

GAZPACHO

ACAI BOWL WITH CHIA & TOASTED COCONUT

PULLED JACKFRUIT TACOS

DAY 27

WEEK 4
SATURDAY

Check the ingredients on the tin of baked beans to make sure they are vegan. Make extra for tonight for a quick leftovers lunch tomorrow.

Baked beans on toast

SERVES: 1
PREP / COOK TIME
5 minutes / 10 minutes

1 French shallot, finely chopped
½ tablespoon red wine vinegar
8 oz tinned baked beans
½ teaspoon chili flakes
½ oz baby spinach leaves
1 slice sourdough bread, toasted, to serve

01 In a pan, fry shallot in vinegar for a few minutes to soften. Add beans, 3½ fl oz water and chili flakes and simmer for 8–10 minutes until liquid has reduced down. Stir through spinach and serve on toast.

Nutrition per serving:
621 cals / 4.31g fat / 98.77g carbs / 26.18g protein

Pearl barley with nectarine

SERVES: 1
PREP / COOK TIME
10 minutes / 40 minutes

1¾ oz pearl barley
1 cup water or Vegan broth (p.30)
1 garlic clove, crushed
1 nectarine, sliced
2 tablespoons Sauerkraut (p.20)
¼ oz mint leaves, roughly chopped
¾ oz flaked almonds
1 tablespoon olive oil
juice of ½ lemon
sea salt and pepper

01 In a small pan, add barley, water or broth, garlic and pinch of salt. Bring to the boil, then reduce heat, cover and simmer for 35–40 minutes. Check halfway to make sure there is still enough water over barley. If there is too much liquid left over, drain at end, then cover pan and leave to rest for 5–10 minutes to absorb any remaining liquid. Mix remaining ingredients through barley, season and serve.

Nutrition per serving:
502 cals / 24.69g fat / 64.98g carbs / 11.6g protein

Cauliflower steak with hummus & kale

SERVES: 1
PREP / COOK TIME
5 minutes / 25 minutes

½ head cauliflower
1 curly kale stem, leaves chopped
1 tablespoon olive oil
½ teaspoon ground cumin
3 tablespoons Beet hummus (p.40)
1 tablespoon Roasted sumac chickpeas (p.24)
1 tablespoon Crunchy seed mix (p.24)
sea salt and pepper

01 Preheat oven to 350°F. Cut a ¾–1¼ inch thick slice from the middle of cauliflower. Cut remaining cauliflower into florets. In a bowl, combine florets, kale, half the oil and cumin. Season and toss to coat. Lay cauliflower steak on a lined baking tray. Brush with rest of oil and season. Add florets and kale to another tray. Roast for 20 minutes. Increase oven to 400°F for last 5 minutes. Reserve some cauliflower. Lay rest of florets on top of hummus and steak. Sprinkle with chickpeas and seed mix.

Nutrition per serving:
259 cals / 18.32g fat / 20.32g carbs / 7.08g protein

BAKED BEANS ON TOAST

PEARL BARLEY WITH NECTARINE

CAULIFLOWER STEAK WITH HUMMUS & KALE

DAY 28

WEEK 4

SUNDAY

This breakfast wrap is quite filling and will keep you fuelled for a good part of the day. Freeze left-over ratatouille for another time.

Breakfast tofu & black bean wrap

SERVES: 1
PREP / COOK TIME
5 minutes / 10 minutes

2 teaspoons coconut oil
1 French shallot, thinly sliced
1 garlic clove, crushed
1 small roma (plum) tomato, diced
3½ oz extra firm tofu, grated
3½ oz tinned black beans
1½ oz tinned sweetcorn kernels
¼ oz cilantro, chopped
1 large tortilla wrap
sea salt

01 Heat oil in a frying pan over medium heat and fry shallot and garlic for 2 minutes. Add tomato and cook for 5–6 minutes so tomato softens. Add tofu, black beans, sweetcorn and cilantro and season well. Stir to mix through, then remove from heat and pile into center of tortilla wrap. Fold up bottom and roll wrap to secure filling inside.

Nutrition per serving:
546 cals / 21.79g fat / 63.61g carbs / 30.52g protein

Quinoa jackfruit bowl

SERVES: 1
PREP / COOK TIME
10 minutes / 15 minutes

1½ oz quinoa, rinsed
5½ oz left-over pulled jackfruit (p.114)
¼ oz red cabbage, thinly sliced
1 small carrot, cut into matchsticks
1 scallion, sliced
½ green apple, cut into matchsticks
¼ oz flat-leaf parsley, chopped
¼ oz mint, chopped
½ tablespoon black or white sesame seeds
2 tablespoons Coconut yogurt lime chili dressing (p.18)

01 Place quinoa in a pan and cover with ½ cup water. Bring to the boil, then cover, reduce heat slightly and simmer for 10 minutes. Turn off heat, stir quinoa, then cover and leave to stand for 5–10 minutes.

02 Meanwhile, reheat left-over jackfruit and combine vegetables and herbs to make a slaw-style salad. Serve in a bowl with quinoa and sesame seeds, drizzled with the dressing.

Nutrition per serving:
406 cals / 6.02g fat / 84.11g carbs / 9.68g protein

Ratatouille

SERVES: 2
PREP / COOK TIME
10 minutes / 35 minutes

½ small eggplant, cut into chunks
½ red bell pepper, roughly chopped
1 tablespoon olive oil
1 garlic clove, finely diced
1 French shallot, finely diced
1 zucchini, sliced
½ teaspoon dried mixed herbs
8–10 basil leaves, torn
14 oz tinned diced tomatoes
sea salt and pepper

01 Preheat oven to 350°F. Combine eggplant and bell pepper on a baking tray and drizzle half the oil over. Season and roast for 15–20 minutes. Heat remaining oil in a pan and fry garlic and shallot for a few minutes. Add zucchini, dried herbs and half the basil and cook for 3–4 minutes. Add tomatoes, roasted vegetables and ½ cup water. Season and stir to combine well. Bring to the boil, then reduce heat and simmer for 15 minutes until vegetables have softened. Taste to check seasoning and serve with remaining basil.

Nutrition per serving:
413 cals / 16.02g fat / 59.57g carbs / 12.32g protein

BREAKFAST TOFU & BLACK BEAN WRAP

QUINOA JACKFRUIT BOWL

RATATOUILLE

RECIPE INDEX

A
Acai bowl with chia & toasted coconut 114
Almond butter & banana toast 110
Almond milk 8, 52
Almond milk & pistachio porridge 58
Apple cider detox soda 46
Aquafaba 14
Avocado & sauerkraut chickpea crêpe 84
Avocado pesto toasts 64

B
Baked beans on toast 116
Baked brown rice pudding with peaches 64
Banana bread loaf 34
Banana pancakes 86
Barbecued tofu with bok choy & broccolini 64
Bean shakshuka with cilantro 74
Beet hummus 40
Best green smoothie 66
Bircher muesli 78
Blueberry chia pudding 60
Breakfast tofu & black bean wrap 118
Brown rice herb salad 58
Butter lettuce miso salad 70

C
Candied nuts 24
Carrot & parsnip loaf 34
Carrot & parsnip loaf with cinnamon tahini spread 62
Carrot & parsnip loaf with peanut butter 106
Cauliflower steak with hummus & kale 116
Chargrilled eggplant & sumac dip 40
Charred beans & broccolini tahini salad 94
Chermoula 28
Chia seed crackers 38
Chia seed egg 14
Chickpea flour crêpes 36
Chocolate peanut slice 44
Chutneys 22
Coconut noodle soup with chili & lime 86
Coconut sticky rice pudding 108
Coconut yogurt lime chili dressing 18
Cold drinks 46

Cold soba noodle salad 82
Crackers 38
Creamy dressings 18
Crêpes with mixed berry coulis 100
Crunchy seed mix 24

D
Dips 40

E
Egg alternatives 14
Eggplant caponata 22
Eggplant pizzette 58

F
Falafel plate 78
Fennel & apple Asian slaw with sesame 92
Fennel tea 48
Flatbreads 36, 51
Flaxseed egg 14
Fresh pesto pasta 70

G
Garlic whip 26
Gazpacho 114
Ginger ice tea 46
Granola 32
Granola bars 44
Granola cup 92
Granola with pecans & prunes 112
Guacamole 40

H
Hash browns with spinach & avocado 70
Hot drinks 48
Hot turmeric latte 48

K
Kale & mixed mushroom toasts 82
Kimchi fried quinoa 102

L
Lemon mustard vinaigrette 16
Lemon romaine salad 106
Lentil burgers 100
Lentil pilaf with flaked almonds & herbs 96
Lentil rissoles with tomato & chili relish & cucumber raita 66
Lentil vegetable soup 108

M
Mango smoothie bowl 84
Minced tofu lettuce cups 110
Miso 48
Miso soup with kimchi 74
Miso-glazed eggplant 98
Mixed berry on-the-go smoothie 94
Mixed sprout salad 76

O
Olive oil crackers 38
Olive tapenade 28

P
Pearl barley with nectarine 116
Pesto 26
Piccalilli 20
Piccalilli snack plate 100
Pickles 20
Pico de gallo 28
Polenta fries 42
Pulled jackfruit tacos 114
Pumpernickel with hummus & cucumber 78

Q
Quick flatbread 36
Quick loaves 34
Quick white bean salad 86
Quinoa, asparagus & roasted tomato salad 98
Quinoa banana porridge 96
Quinoa jackfruit bowl 118
Quinoa Mex bowl 76
Quinoa tabbouleh 66

R
Rainbow rice paper rolls with satay sauce 60
Ratatouille 118
Red lentil dal 62
Red wine vinaigrette 16
Rice salad with olives & almonds 112
Roasted cauliflower salad 74
Roasted squash & carrot soup 82
Roasted squash with eggplant dip 102
Roasted stone fruit crumble 80
Roasted sumac chickpeas 24
Rye snaps 38

S
Salsas 28
Salted caramel bliss balls 44
Sauerkraut 20
Sesame rice wine dressing 16
Sesame tofu stir-fry 60
Simple kale salad 80
Simple nut butter 8
Spiced roasted nuts 42
Spreads 26
Squash curry 94
Strawberry cordial 46
Stuffed portobello mushrooms 68
Summer fruit salad 98
Sushi hand rolls 90
Sweet pickled celery & fennel 20
Sweet potato muffins 76
Sweet snacks 44

T
Toasted banana bread 90
Tofu & spinach saag 96
Tofu cream cheese 26
Tofu laksa 112
Tofu miso dressing 18
Tofu miso red cabbage slaw 108
Tofu scramble 68
Tomato & chili relish 22
Tomato salad with garlic croutons 68

V
Vegan aïoli 18
Vegan broth 30
Vegan meatloaf 106
Vegetable bake 92
Vegetable chips 42
Vegetable gyoza with bok choy 80
Vinaigrette dressings 16

W
Warm beet & walnut salad 62
Warm lentil watercress salad 84
Warm roasted root vegetables with chermoula 90
Wild rice with mixed mushrooms & kale 110

Z
Zucchini & corn cakes with pico de gallo 102